Pengu:

Princess THE Bitchface SYNDROME

Dr Michael Carr-Gregg is one of Australia's highest profile psychologists and an internationally recognised authority on teenage behaviour. He was the founder of the world's first national support group for teenage cancer patients, CanTeen, and has been Executive Director of the New Zealand Drug Foundation, Associate Professor at the University of Melbourne's Department of Paediatrics and a political lobbyist. He is currently a consultant psychologist to many schools and national organisations, including Reach Out and beyondblue. He has been a regular on Melbourne radio 3 AW, the resident parenting expert on Channel 7's *Sunrise* since 2005 and a regular on its *Morning Show*. He has written several bestselling books on parenting, including *Surviving Adolescents* and *Beyond Cyberbullying*, and is the 'Agony Uncle' for *Girlfriend* magazine. He has won many awards for his work.

THE Princess Bitchface SYNDROME

Surviving adolescent girls

MICHAEL CARR-GREGG

ILLUSTRATIONS BY RON TANDBERG

Penguin Books

PENGUIN BOOKS

UK | USA | Canada | Ireland | Australia
India | New Zealand | South Africa | China

Penguin Books is part of the Penguin Random House group of companies
whose addresses can be found at global.penguinrandomhouse.com.

Penguin
Random House
Australia

First published by Penguin Group (Australia), 2006

Text copyright © Michael Carr-Gregg 2006
Illustrations copyright © Ron Tandberg 2006

The moral right of the author has been asserted

Design by Karen Trump © Penguin Group (Australia)
Illustrations by Ron Tandberg
Typeset in Simoncini Garamond by Post Pre-press Group, Brisbane, Queensland
Printed and bound in Australia by McPherson's Printing Group, Maryborough, Victoria

National Library of Australia
Cataloguing-in-Publication data:

Carr-Gregg, Michael.
The princess bitchface syndrome: surviving adolescent girls.
Includes index.
ISBN 978 0 14 300466 0.
1. Teenage girls. 2. Parent and teenager. 3. Adolescent
psychology. I. Title.

305.235

www.penguin.com.au

To Thérèse

'Mother Nature is providential. She gives us twelve years to develop a love for our children before turning them into teenagers.' William Galvin

'The two worst years of a woman's life are the year she is 13 and the year her daughter is.' Nell Minow

Contents

A mother's story

I think I would call her the stranger who arrived to replace the other person we knew – we now have the both of them living with us in one person happily. Her key characteristics were an absolute will of iron, able to undertake secret missions, able to self-destruct at a moment's notice, moods like Melbourne's weather, able to home in on my own concerns about my parenting, use my own words and display any number of my own characteristics.

I was her main target and she would hurt me terribly, mostly deliberately, and sometimes inadvertently. Her aim was to be her own person in any way she wanted, regardless. The air was fraught with enormous emotional storms. She was thoughtless about the effort people put in, and her own worst enemy in terms of not doing what would seem to be a good idea.

Opposition was at all costs until we were all exhausted, but I had no idea what she would do next – just the opposite of anything we came up with. This daughter was delineating herself almost desperately and I think she was also confused. She would remain loving when the storm blew through, and meant well.

I think she was frightened by the world and her own power. She was confounded by and resented her sister's time of strife later – which incidentally was nowhere near as difficult for me – it was more of a passive resistance and the argument was between the sisters. I had given up resisting and suggesting, something I had learnt from the earlier experience. I also sympathised with both, but did not comment on either party. It was eight years of hell and even writing about it now I find that we remember events differently – it is as if they were different incidents or times for both of us. I think moving house, spending too much time at work and having my elderly parents (who were ill at times) in the house made it harder for all the family.

However, she fought with Grandma too on one occasion and I remember being between the two of them while they were arguing, and hearing myself from two eras thinking in support of one, 'Good point'; and then supporting the other – thinking, 'Yes, that's true, too.' It was like two parts of me, or two voices I could relate to.

Introduction

Many people picking up this book for the first time might find its title distasteful. So I feel the need to explain where it came from – an experience recounted to me by a 30-something friend of mine called Nikki, who was enjoying a fairly 'robust' relationship with her teenage daughter. Nikki was particularly envious of a friend who insisted on waxing lyrical about how quiet, helpful and studious her own adolescent was. Then one day Nikki attended a school morning tea and, with a slightly heavy heart expecting the usual rant, ambled over to the mother of this paragon of virtues and asked politely how her daughter was. Nikki was more than a little surprised at the response: 'You mean Princess Bitchface?'

Clearly, the puberty fairy had arrived and left a very special type of teenager under this parent's pillow . . .

Of course, there are plenty of teenage girls who rise early, shower and get ready for the day without being disagreeable. But listen to parents and teachers, as I do on a regular basis, and you would have to agree that there are indisputably some girls whose behaviour seems for a period of time like a direct emotional assault.

So, is it just teenage girls who behave in this manner? Well, pretty much. The reality is that while young boys often start off by being more demanding and labour-intensive than girls, there is no doubt that girls reach higher levels of complication as they get older. Many parents discover how difficult parenting really can be when their daughters hit puberty and become entwined in intricate adolescent peer relationships, which can have a domino effect on the home front. Teenage boys tend to be less involved in emotional complexities.

I've decided to call this manifestation 'the Princess Bitchface Syndrome'. In psychology, the word 'syndrome' refers to a collection of signs or symptoms that together form a condition with a known outcome, or which requires a special response. In my view, precisely such a collection of signs and/or symptoms exists not just in the Australian community but across the western world – an instantly recognisable adolescent female who transforms almost overnight into a rebellious stranger who behaves like a responsible adult one day and a spoiled child the next.

❀

Talkback radio switchboards across Australia neared meltdown in February 2006 after two 14-year-old girls were charged with dragging a disabled 53-year-old taxi driver from his cab, bashing him to death and stealing his vehicle and mobile phone. The girls were also allegedly involved in an armed robbery a day after his death. Where, it was plaintively asked, were their parents, and what were these girls doing wandering around the suburbs of Sydney at 2 a.m.?

In the past decade, boys have (for good reason) grabbed the psychological limelight. Yet you don't need to be the Agony Uncle for a teenage girls' magazine to realise that life for our young women is tougher now than ever before. Divorce rates are up to almost 50 per cent, the average length of new marriages is 11 years, and the number of children in care has jumped 70 per cent over the last decade because of increased reports of neglect and abuse. One in four young women has been a victim of drink-spiking and/or sexual molestation. Anxiety and depression rates are rising too: 11 per cent of our girls routinely engage in deliberate self-harm, and underage drinking kills one teenager and results in more than 60 hospital admissions each week.

Planet Girl is in crisis. There is something terribly wrong when, in counselling sessions, 13-year-old girls wring their hands about whether they are satisfying their sexual partner, or when 10-year-olds write to magazines reporting that they have lost their virginity and can't understand why 'he' doesn't return their calls. By the time girls turn 13 they look like they're ready for anything. But they're not.

As a society we appear to be losing it when it comes to parenting our girls. More and more young women seem to be in charge of their own lives, more worried about pleasing their age peers than listening to or respecting their parents. Right across Australia, battle-weary parents are raising the white flag and beating a hasty retreat from the fray.

Every week in my office I witness girls who are empowered to the point where the adults in their lives feel helpless and ineffectual. Adolescents' wish lists become must-do lists, because to deprive a child of an iPod (let alone make them attend a 'boring' family function, church or carol service) is seen by many as akin to cruelty, neglect and abuse. This generation is enmeshed in a culture of getting and spending – and there can be double trouble where parents have divorced, separated or blended, because if one parent doesn't buy for the child, the other will.

In the current environment, it is politically incorrect to suggest that parents are responsible for this state of affairs – because this is 'parent bashing' and induces guilt. But surely we have an obligation to make healthy choices that will guide our daughters, socialise them and eventually teach them to be independent. If we don't perform this role, who will?

This book, then, is about parenting with intelligence, with a loving but firm hand. While it is counterproductive for parents to be in the faces of their daughters 24/7, it is vital that you are supportive, make them feel safe, valued and trusted and, above all, that you know where they are, who they are with and what they are doing. This applies to young people of both genders, of course: they need boundaries and rules if they are to learn right from wrong.

You cannot parent the most vulnerable generation of teenagers in our history via mobile phone. In other words, it is time to get a plan, develop a strategy and get involved.

Chapter 1

A crash course in developmental psychology

Before I attempt to explain the Princess Bitchface Syndrome, it is worth doing some scene-setting. Australia today has around 3–3.5 million young people going through puberty/adolescence at any one time, depending on how you define those terms.

Understanding adolescence

Generally, puberty refers to the physical changes that transform a child into a sexually developed being, while adolescence is a catch-all term for the other changes – emotional, psychological, social – that follow in its wake. Puberty is mother nature's hormone titration experiment, whereby the brain and pituitary gland release hormones that regulate the reproductive organs of both males and females. As a result children begin to mature biologically, psychologically, socially and cognitively – a process that can take anywhere from one year to six. Everyone matures at their own pace, but eventually they all catch up. When looked at from a simple biological viewpoint this all sounds pretty straightforward, but many parents find this time both baffling and frustrating. Let me give you an example.

Doug is driving home after a long day at work. He is 40-something, runs a flourishing business and has spent his entire day in a very successful board meeting. As he eases through the traffic, he's feeling quietly satisfied – the board is pleased with his management of the company and the 50-odd staff members. He's received a bonus, some important new initiatives have been given the green light, and his mood has been further improved by a few beers in the pub afterwards.

Doug parks his car and walks, with a spring in his step, to the front door. Hanging up his coat he hears a noise emanating from the living room, and poking his head around the door he sees his 12-year-old daughter Chloe, feet up on the sofa, watching

The OC. Doug is at what some adolescent psychologists refer to as 'the moment of truth'. What will he do next? He could walk over to Chloe, tousle her hair and say, 'Hi, darling, how was your day? What's Seth up to?' But he doesn't. Instead, a voice rises from deep within him, fuelled by a mixture of alcohol and a heritage-listed parenting script, and he strides into the room, glares at his daughter and utters the six words guaranteed to elicit a defensive response from any teenager: 'Chloe, have you done your homework?'

Chloe has had a reasonably good day and is in an unusually genial mood. Only mildly irritated at the lack of a warm greeting and the provocative question, she chooses to ignore her father's inquiry and says nothing. She is hoping her silence will be taken as a non-verbal clue – that she doesn't wish to engage in conversation, as at this moment she is clearly engrossed in something far more important to her. Something, in fact, that will most likely be the sole topic of conversation on the train tomorrow morning. Doug, sadly, doesn't get the hint. Undeterred by her silence, he walks a little closer to the fruit of his loins and delving into the university of the bleeding obvious, asks in a louder voice, 'Are you deaf?' It is a silly question, as he knows the answer.

Chloe, more irritated now, sighs and emits a neanderthal grunt – providing a further opportunity for her father to back off and take the conversation in a different direction. But by now Doug is in the mood for a confrontation, and he walks over to the TV and turns it off. Chloe now does a commendable imitation of Mt Vesuvius, gets off the sofa, tells her father to go forth and multiply and, in time-honoured tradition, storms out of the house, slamming the door (for added effect) and yelling to her mother that she's going to her best friend's place to watch the rest of the program with 'normal' people. Doug is left standing alone, in the now silent room, wondering what he has done wrong. He pours himself a whiskey, downs it and walks into the kitchen where Caroline, his wife of 17 years, and their 10-year-old son William, are preparing the evening meal. Instead of the standard 'Honey, I'm home' greeting, he demands, 'Did you hear that?' Caroline has indeed heard the confrontation, one of many in recent times, and she sighs and says, 'Everyone heard it'.

'Well, she can't talk to me like that!' he replies.

'Well, she just did!' says Caroline.

'We'll see about that!' Doug says, grabbing his keys and heading off to his car to search for his daughter. But when he gets to the bottom of the road, to his dismay he discovers a booze bus has just been set up. He is breathalysed and loses his licence.

So what went wrong? This man – like millions of his counterparts across Australia and elsewhere – lacks what is known in psychological circles as a 'developmental perspective'. A new set of skills, knowledge and strategies are needed to parent the 'new' adolescent. Doug needs to know that all young people need some 'staring into the fire' time after school – that the secret of harmonius communication with teenagers is to avoid language that triggers their inherent sensitivity to control. He must discard his old parenting script and learn a new one (see chapter 4 for more on this), one which recognises that during adolescence it is not just the body that undergoes tectonic changes, but the brain is also transformed. When Doug speaks to Chloe, he should remember that her brain is a work in progress and won't be fully formed for maybe another decade. He needs to take into account that he is dealing with a unique species – the adolescent – not a miniature version of himself. He needs to understand that Chloe doesn't act like an adult because she doesn't think like an adult. She's an adolescent.

So what is adolescence? It is best understood as a transitional period between childhood and adulthood, characterised by physical and psychological changes that do not occur on a strict timeline but at different times according to a genetic roadmap unique to each individual. This is by definition a period of flux which, while perfectly normal in theory, can in practice produce confusion and discord. Common issues identified by adolescent girls include conflicts with parents and siblings, concerns about peers and peer relationships, concerns about school and concerns about their physical safety.

Though adolescence has long been a more or less challenging time for both teenagers and parents, 21st-century life has added some new ingredients to the mix. While these are not limited to girls, their generally superior communication skills (sharply honed in the primary-school playground) tend to make them more articulate than their male counterparts about what's going on in their lives.

How her brain develops

At birth Chloe had more than 100 billion brain cells, more than there are stars in the Milky Way. In newborns, only about 17 per cent of these cells are interconnected (these connections are responsible for the functioning of the autonomic nervous system, which directs our heartbeat and breathing, controls reflexes, and regulates other basic functions). The brain continues to form connections over the next two decades, in fits and starts, by adding grey matter (neurones, dendrites and synapses) and pruning old synapses, destroying old neural connections and building new ones – all the time producing the complex circuits that shape our thinking, feelings and behaviour. Chloe and her adolescent counterparts are navigating a cerebral cyclone, without a map or compass.

Recent brain research has improved our understanding of adolescent girls. It seems that few organs are as gender-specific as the human brain: magnetic resonance imaging (MRI) has shown that in girls the corpus callosum (a bundle of fibres between the left and the right hemispheres) has approximately 30 per cent more connections than is the case with boys. In other words, the female brain is more integrated, allowing both brain hemispheres to work together; in addition, the limbic system, which controls emotions, is more active in the female brain, so that thoughts and emotions are more intertwined.

For decades, developmental psychologists assumed that the adolescent brain was fully formed when the skull reached adult size – by the age of 13 or 14. But a few years ago a US neuroscientist, Dr Jay Geidd, discovered that there was a second growth spurt – another overproduction of grey matter – just before puberty, followed by a second bout of neural Darwinism ('use-it-or-lose-it') pruning during adolescence itself. Pruning allows the brain to invest in strengthening the connections that the individual finds most necessary and important. If your daughter does a lot of reading, she will become a better reader; if she plays the piano a great deal when young, she will become a better pianist. What they use and learn in school will become hard-wired into the brain's structure – but what they ignore will lose its priority.

It is important to be aware that the brain's centre of reasoning and problem-solving, the prefrontal cortex, is the last to mature, and that the brain is not fully developed until the early 20s. To compensate for this shortfall, the adolescent relies heavily on another area of the brain, the amygdala, the primitive and instinctive part, which creates a tendency to react automatically. In other words, adolescents do not have the same ability as adults to control their impulses and make sound decisions, which in turn means there is no point in judging their actions from an adult perspective – to do so is both unfair and unhelpful, and will inevitably lead to disappointment.

Other research has shown that the myelin sheaths that insulate nerve fibres in the brain are also still developing in adolescence. This is the process during which neurons and dendrites become coated with a fatty substance (myelin) to enable neural impulses to travel faster. Just as a bare electrical cable, without plastic insulation, allows some electricity to escape and so loses power, the uninsulated adolescent brain transmits signals much more slowly than that of a fully mature adult. This is also likely to contribute to the often-observed teenage trait of finding it hard to quickly think through the consequences of an action or to control their emotions.

The Insurance Institute for Highway Safety in the US found that the highest scores on the sensation-seeking scale come around age 16, with the dangerous period ending when young people's control centres reach maturity – around age 25. Another factor contributing to impulsiveness is the fact that teens' hormones begin pushing them into more risky, thrill-seeking behaviours. And last but by no means least, adolescents are by nature particularly prey to peer pressure, often, for example, driving more dangerously when they have friends with them. The Insurance Institute says the probability of a car crash doubles if a driver under 18 has two peers in the vehicle; if there are three or more, it quadruples. US psychologist Lawrence Steinberg, a specialist in the field of adolescent health and development, conducted research into this phenomenon and in one test found that adolescents playing a video car game drove 30 per cent faster when they had friends with them.

Even the judicial system is sitting up and taking notice of such discoveries as these. In March 2005 the US Supreme Court held that the Eighth and Fourteenth Amendments forbade the execution of offenders under the age of 18. This fresh understanding does not excuse juvenile offenders from punishment for violent crime, but it lessens their culpability.

With all this restructuring, is it any wonder that the teenage brain is at times disorganised, impulsive and prone to misinterpretation? Above all, these facts should underscore for parents of adolescents the importance of being an understanding voice of reason, of strategically setting limits and boundaries, and of consequential learning (see chapters 4 and 5).

Rites of passage

As I said in my book *Surviving Adolescents*, it is natural for young people to seek psychological separation, independence and 'a sense of self' at this stage of their lives. This is both a biological and emotional imperative. But this rite of passage is, just as naturally, complicated by the fact that they are *not* yet fully grown and that their brain is a work in progress.

Adolescence has always been that in-between time when, to quote pop princess Britney Spears: 'I'm not a girl. Not yet a woman.'

In the grey zone between childhood and adulthood, Chloe too is caught between the past and the future. Although biologically mature, in that she is capable of sexual reproduction, psychologically and socially she has still not achieved adulthood. This has not always been the case. The notion of adolescence being a distinct developmental process is a relatively new phenomenon in western societies, a byproduct of the Industrial Revolution, prior to which young people went straight from childhood to adulthood once they were old enough to procreate or to go to work.

In some cultures there is a formal age of maturity, when young people are deemed to become adults. For example, in the Jewish tradition females are considered to be adult members of the community at age 12, and this transition is celebrated in the Bat Mitzvah (the Bar Mitzvah, the equivalent ceremony for boys, is held at age 13). Amongst Australian Aborigines, girls were traditionally married when they reached puberty, before which they were ceremonially prepared by the other women in the tribal group.

I believe there is much to be recommended in such traditions: without a ritual that says 'Now you are an adult', the rapid biological changes of puberty can engender confusion, uncertainty and 'status anxiety'. In Australia, 'Schoolies Week' seems to have become the default rite of passage for many young people at the end of their last school year, with thousands of young people heading for coastal towns to celebrate the end of their exams and the beginning of their new-found freedom. Sadly, excessive use of alcohol and other drugs seems to have become an indispensable component of the festivities.

Where have all the children gone?

Today, puberty occurs earlier than ever before – around age 10, according to the World Health Organization. For the vast majority of Australian girls, it is a transition with a fairly predictable sequence of physical changes: the release of increased quantities of hormones produces an overall growth spurt, the ovaries become active, breasts and body hair develop, and menstruation starts. Unlike the slow progress experienced in childhood, change is now rapid and dramatic. One difference between girls and boys at this point is that girls commonly undergo the general growth spurt before or around the same time that they begin to develop sexually, whereas boys tend to acquire their 'secondary' sexual characteristics first and grow taller later. For girls, a key challenge of adolescence is to adjust to this new physical self: she looks less like a child and more like a young woman, with the result that she often becomes extremely focused on her body. She needs to incorporate in her unfolding self-image a sense of what it means to be female, she needs to develop a set of values about sexual behaviour, and she must learn to manage her sexuality (I discuss this in more detail in chapter 6).

For all young people, female or male, adolescence is also a time to begin separating from their parents, to break the emotional ties that have bound them to Mum and Dad up until now. For most of them, this shift involves engaging in one or more risk-taking behaviours – so much so that this may be seen as a normal developmental process. In the majority of cases, fortunately, they gradually develop a capacity for self-discipline and can assess which behaviours are acceptable and safe.

Over the last few years, assisted by a constant barrage of sexual images and lyrics, childhood as we knew it seems to have been steadily eroded away. There is unprecedented pressure on young people to grow up much earlier. Many girls today seem to be going straight from toys to boys, without a stop at the 'tween' years. They can't drive or vote, but have been raised as consumers: they have a significant disposable income and form the most powerful consumer group since the baby boom.

Chloe, who we met earlier in this chapter, is a typical tween. When her mother was 12, she was dreaming about ponies and married bliss with Donny Osmond, and dressed quite differently to teenage girls. Chloe, on the other hand, is being sold the same clothes as 18-year-olds: she's into push-up bras, thong underwear, and low-rider jeans. She wears eyeliner and mascara, displays a bare midriff, listens to sexually explicit rap lyrics and her favourite TV show, as we have seen, is *The OC*. Chloe has grown up so fast that she's really missed out on what Freud called 'the latency period' – a kind of waiting-room for girls en route to the teen years. She is fashion-conscious, fad-loving and very vocal – full of 'attitude'. At her 12th birthday party there was no jumping castle, no traditional games such as pass the parcel or musical chairs, and no little girls in frilly dresses. Her friends turned up dressed as 21st-century pop-divas sporting denim mini-skirts, sparkly satin or faux-leather pants, flirty or cropped tops, and platform-heel knee-high boots. In copying Beyoncé's skimpy, provocative outfits, they have no idea what the sexual impact is – just because their bodies are maturing, it doesn't mean their minds are too. Parents who allow early adolescents to follow such fads should think about what message they are sending about body image.

Lastly, at Chloe's party there were no Barbie dolls as gifts – nowadays, even 8-year-olds deem dolls and other playthings babyish. Indeed, a UK study in 2005 revealed that girls aged 7–11 felt such hostility towards the Barbie dolls of their earlier childhood that they were 'torturing, maiming and even decapitating' them.

So, long before puberty proper has hit, Chloe's posters of cute puppies and ponies, along with her own drawings, have come off the bedroom wall and been replaced with images of celebrities. Every six weeks or so, Chloe's mother treats her to a $60 haircut and an $80 facial; she also has the occasional pedicure and manicure. Chloe wields significant influence over her parent's purse-strings, too, known by marketers as 'pester power', with early adolescents influencing more than 67 per cent of all brands their parents buy, including the family home and car, and even where they holiday. And in choosing her secondary school, one of Chloe's friends based her shortlist on the ones with the coolest uniforms.

What, then, are the characteristics of today's 'typical' teenage adolescent girl? Following is a broad guide to the developmental stages, though it's important to remember that each girl's passage through each stage is determined not only by biological growth and change, but also by temperament and personality, adult expectations and social influences. This generation is more media-savvy than any preceding one and has been raised on images of sassy but strong 'girl heroes'. At the same time, today's ideal stick-thin look can cause body-image problems: statistics show that one in 100 Australian girls aged 12–19 develops the eating disorder anorexia nervosa and close to one in 20 develops bulimia.

Early adolescence

Early adolescence roughly corresponds to ages 10–15. Chloe, whose bones, muscles and organs have grown unevenly – resulting in the classic gangly look of this age-group – feels gawky and sometimes looks awkward as well. Like most early adolescents she is progressing through puberty and is intensely conscious of the physical changes she's undergoing, particularly when she compares herself with her peers, which serves to increase her anxiety about her body shape, her growth and her sexuality. She's become very sensitive to teasing about her appearance and needs buckets of reassurance that she's normal.

Chloe vacillates between wanting to turn away from her childhood and the authority of her parents, and needing to feel free to depend on them. She has rapid mood swings and can become easily upset and emotional, alternating between extreme cooperation and extreme resistance to adult guidance. There is no shortage of low-voltage conflict, most often centring on sibling rivalry and normal developmental forgetfulness with respect to jobs around the house, homework, and her bedroom (which often looks as if the SAS has been training in it).

Chloe's parents have noticed that she has progressed from fairly concrete thinking towards logical thought and has a limited ability to extend logic to abstract concepts. She still has difficulty identifying how her immediate behaviour impacts upon her future. She scorns the imaginative and illogical thinking of her early childhood, but spends much time and energy accumulating general knowledge and has developed an ability to apply learned concepts to new tasks.

While still fairly egocentric, Chloe is slowly developing a conscience, moving from a 'What's in it for me?' approach ('If I do this for you, what will you do for me?') to a desire to gain social approval and live up to the expectations of people close to her (for example, she may place the needs of others over her own self-interest). Sadly, this new perspective is not always reflected in her behaviour, as can be seen from the emotional violence ('relational aggression', as psychologists call it) she and her peers engage in at school.

Chloe's sense of self is heavily influenced by her relationships with parents and siblings, teachers and, increasingly, peers. The close friendships formed by early adolescent girls are best understood as intense little love affairs, usually based on geographical proximity (though mobiles and internet chatting have made this less important), shared interests and hobbies, or other connections. They tend to have fewer, but emotionally closer, friends than boys do (for more on cliques, see chapter 3), and shifting peer alliances are common as one girl matures faster or slower than others.

Her predominant psychological need is to develop a sense of mastery and accomplishment, to be seen as capable. She feels it is still okay to learn skills from her parents, especially her mother, and to make and fix things. At the same time, her relatively slow brain development ensures a tendency to be disorganised and forgetful.

So, what has Chloe to expect in the coming years?

Middle adolescence

In middle adolescence (around 14–17 years old) girls have more mobility and independence and, as a result, there is less adult presence and protection in their lives.

She wants to be as grown-up as possible. Her childhood icons have been replaced by mobile phones and the internet, TV soaps and 'teen' comedies, and glamorous, raunchy pop singers and celebs. Her taste in magazines runs from *Girlfriend* and *Dolly* to *Cosmopolitan* and *Cleo*. The emotional temperature in the home rises as tensions between family over autonomy become more and more frequent. Many of her friends are drinking alcohol regularly and several have used illicit drugs at least once in the past year.

She is in the process of developing new intellectual powers, such as thinking in abstract terms, thinking more about possibilities, thinking more about the very process of thinking. She is thinking in multiple dimensions, and seeing in shades of grey rather than simply in black and white. She does not always feel

'Our 14-year-old daughter seems rational and reasonable one minute, but the next she's quite a pain. She just doesn't seem to listen to us any more. She forgets things we've asked her to do and accuses us of nagging when we remind her. One day we have a decent conversation with her and we think "Great! That stage has passed." But then two days later, she'll be acting like a child again.'

Your daughter is not necessarily being deliberately obnoxious. As a parent it's helpful to see this as a manifestation of the natural development going on in her brain, of which inconsistency is one of the symptoms. Her brain is trying to sort through lots of options and identities – whether she's going to be an academic, an athlete or an artist. Our job is to ensure that the choices she makes don't have irreversible consequences. We need to develop a tolerance of the more relatively minor missteps, and not forget that it is also frustrating for the girls themselves – they don't *choose* to be defiant or disobedient or disorganised.

the need to squander precious minutes on thinking ahead or weighing up the consequences of her actions. Relationships have a distinctly self-centred quality, which can be intensely irritating to her parents, as is her tendency to lose things. If her parents are not careful, she's likely to play them like a fiddle.

Although she is still self-focused she is very concerned about what others, particularly her peers, think of her. Her need for peer-group acceptance is so great that at school she checks the popularity barometer daily, as gaining and retaining social approval is paramount. She has a growing desire for privacy and is sensitive about the changes her body is undergoing (breasts, periods, and so on). Her parents are noticing frequent mood swings, especially when she spends too much time alone. She seeks to prove her individuality by spurning adult control and support, often resulting in significant levels of conflict. Her new thinking abilities may be evidenced in the use of sarcasm and in arguing with her parents and other authority figures, which may result in further clashes. Her obsessive focus on peer friendships may also lead her to reject physical affection at home, which can be distressing. She has greater interest in making her own decisions and benefits from more opportunities to do so (within the scope of her current abilities).

Her friendships still begin with perceived commonalities, but increasingly involve the sharing of values and personal confidences. Being part of a clique provides her with a greater sense of security, though antisocial cliques can increase rebellious behaviours at this stage. Romantic crushes are common, as are dating and increased sexual activity.

The process of identity formation is intensifying and she is experimenting increasingly with different roles, looks, values and friendships, and her sexuality. Peer relationships help her explore and develop her own identity. She is becoming surer of her own beliefs and may start making plans for her future. At the same time, body image may still be a central concern and her parents are concerned that her apparent low self-esteem may contribute to an eating disorder.

Late adolescence

Late adolescence refers to the years past high school, from around age 17 into the early twenties.

By now she is physically an adult, and accepted as an adult in her environment. Many of her friends are seeking to pursue further education or vocational training. Her self-image is now more consistent with the realities of her size, shape and abilities, and with societal limits and expectations. She has a well-established sexual identity, and is having satisfying intimate relationships.

Despite her adult appearance, her brain is not fully developed (whatever she might think). She stills needs help associating effort with outcome, and with planning and organising.

She is now much less egocentric and shows increased understanding of abstract values. She can see the bigger societal picture and might value moral principles over laws (known in the trade as 'principled morality'). On the other hand, her differing rates of cognitive and emotional development may mean she will advocate for specific values and violate them at the same time. Her

Early adolescent girls	Middle adolescent girls	Late adolescent girls
Main concerns		
Am I popular?	**Where do I belong?**	**Where am I going?**
Major developmental issues		
Coming to terms with the changes of puberty	Superior intellectual powers	Emancipation from adult caregivers
Struggle to break away from parents, particularly mother	New sexual desires	Realistic body image
Clique relationships crucial	Increased experimentation and risk-taking	Acceptance of sexual identity
Anxiety about body shape and changes	Relationships	Development of educational/vocational goals
Comparisons with peers		Developing intimate relationships
Cognitive development		
Still concrete thinkers	More rational thought	Longer attention span
Less able to understand subtlety	Individual freedom	Abstract thought
Daydreaming common	Accept more responsibility for consequences of choices	Ability to synthesise information
	Take on greater responsibility within family	Able to think into the future
Parental responsibility		
Reassure about normality	Respect need for privacy	Help associate effort with outcome
Make explanations short	Negotiate rules around safety	Help plan goals
Have clear boundaries on issues relating to safety	Reward compliance with more freedom	Help develop strategies

increased ability to empathise with others may mean a further intensification of relationships and a tendency to worry more, with an almost obsessive concern for friends and family, and life problems. Her parents are relieved to see she is generally acting more responsibly. There are fewer conflicts with her parents nowadays and she is beginning to see them as individuals and take their perspectives into account. She is showing interest in taking on 'adult' responsibilities (babysitting, having her own bank account, doing her own laundry, etc.).

These, then, are the chief factors that help explain the inconsistent, sometimes infuriating, behaviour of the 'normal' adolescent girl. On the one hand, adolescence is a time of rapid biological change: she is maturing physically and experiencing new and strange impulses that she doesn't yet know how to handle. On the other hand, although she is biologically mature she is not yet an adult in psychological and social terms. So if she behaves like a grown-up one day and a stubborn child the next, it is because she *is* half-child and half-adult. If she likes one thing one moment and another thing the next, it is because she really doesn't yet know what she wants. If she is rebellious or challenges your values and rules, it is because she is searching for her own coherent, stable sense of self.

Parents need to think of this journey as an economist would. At first you invest your love and energy, and the returns are great. Middle adolescence can sometimes feel like a recession, as you get little or nothing back. But the good news is that towards the end of the journey most parents discover that not only is their original investment still there, on the whole its value has increased immeasurably.

EARLY
ADOLESCENCE

LATE
ADOLESCENCE

TANDBERG

Chapter 2
Times have changed

To add to the more predictable challenges facing contemporary adolescents (and their parents), this is arguably the most vulnerable generation in Australia's history. There are six key factors combining to create a richly nutritious mix in which the seeds of the Princess Bitchface Syndrome can germinate and thrive.

Body and brain development are out of synch

The ever-earlier onset of puberty means that the brain development of young people is lagging further and further behind their physical, cognitive and emotional development (in psychobabble this is known as 'developmental compression'). And as we have seen, girls typically develop physically and sexually sooner than boys.

Many of today's parents grew up in an era when puberty arrived at about 16 years of age, preceded by a 'free-range' childhood

(Freud's 'latency period' when, according to him, children generally identify with the same-sex parent and play with other children of the same sex). In this way young people in the past could learn and practise important social skills (such as anger management, conflict resolution and assertiveness), and gather both physical and psychological strength to explore the world, all within the comfort and safety of their own gender. In other words, they had time to marshall their forces for the arrival of puberty.

Now everything has changed. Research from the UK in 2000 found that around 16 per cent of girls reach puberty by the age of eight; while an American study in 1997 showed it was normal for girls as young as seven to start developing breasts. The ever-earlier onset of puberty has been attributed to all sorts of factors:

- better nutrition, producing greater body mass and fat, which can initiate puberty
- lack of exercise (in very active children, such as gymnasts, puberty starts later)
- stress (girls whose parents divorce, for instance, may start puberty earlier)

- chemicals in food (e.g. hormones fed to chickens).

An assortment of paediatric boffins have identified a number of other possible reasons, including the media-driven sexualisation of children, the disintegration of the nuclear family, and watching too much television. University of Florence Professor Roberto Salti has argued that watching too much TV may distort the hormonal balance of adolescents and push many of them into early puberty. His research team found children denied access to television for just one week experienced a 30 per cent jump in their melatonin levels (this hormone is thought to prevent the early onset of puberty). If confirmed, this would be the first evidence of television-watching having a direct physiological impact on the young.

Owing to the lack of conclusive evidence linking any of the above to the changed timing of puberty, we must assume that a multiplicity of factors is involved. Whatever the reasons, the fact is that as a result many young people today are psychologically under-cooked – which can be seen in rising rates of anxiety, substance misuse and eating disorders, and in some cases depression, self-harm and suicidal thoughts. It seems that many adolescents lack the important life skill of resilience – the capacity to face, overcome and be strengthened by adversity.

To put it simply, the developmental stages have somehow got out of whack. So, as likely as not, you've already been confronted by a fully 'developed' mid-teen, complete with hipster jeans and pierced navel, but with the cognitive capacity of a 10-year-old. A souped-up car with all the extras – but the driver has no licence. Today some young people merely dip their toes ever so briefly in the waters of the latency period, before a combination of external factors (especially peer and media pressures, which are contributing to early sexualisation), lures them prematurely into adolescence. Others go straight from Hi-5 to Beyoncé, bypassing the latency phase altogether.

A decline in social connectedness

The last few years have also seen a decline in 'social capital' – defined by the World Bank as 'the institutions, relationships and norms that shape the quality and quantity of a society's social interactions . . . the glue that holds them together'. Professor Gordon Parker, head of the Royal Prince Alfred's Black Dog Institute (which specialises in mood disorders), says: 'There used to be mooring posts in our community. You grew up with an affiliation in a particular suburb and church. Now mooring posts have become rare. For a while the RSL replaced the church, but what will replace RSLs?' According to US sociologist Professor Robert D. Putnam, getting involved in organised groups or voluntary work can have a significant positive impact on both individuals and community life, making us happier, healthier and more productive. This is particularly relevant for teenage girls, as research by US psychologist Sonya Lyubomirsky suggests that those who do charitable work are happier than those who don't. No doubt for these sorts of reasons, many secondary schools require their students to undertake periodic community work.

Social fragmentation has also resulted in the decline of kinship networks, in part the result of the population shift from the country to urban areas (in 1861, 60 per cent of Australians were rural dwellers; a century later, this figure had fallen to 18 per cent, a dramatic reversal). As elsewhere in the world, the extended families that traditionally sustained and nurtured Australians have dissipated, with the result that many parents no longer have access to the wisdom and support of the previous generation. The situation is compounded by the fact that since the 1970s , relationships have become much more fluid, with a strong emphasis on the individual, a consequent loss of connectedness and commitment and, until the last couple of years, a falling marriage rate.

How has all this impacted on young women? For one thing, there is less consistency in parenting styles, which range from what is, in effect, supervision at a distance – by mobile phone, with parents imposing few or no limits or demands – to children being subjected to unprecedented levels of surveillance and control. The latter approach has resulted from an increasing climate of fear about the risks 'out there' despite the real social evidence, such as a hardly reported ABS survey that showed a significant drop in crime between 2003 and 2004 and an increase in the number of people who reported that their neighbourhoods were crime-free.

'I'm 12 and my parents won't let me do anything! I can't have a conversation without Mum interrupting; I can't go for walks with my friends or be left alone at home too long. All they do is worry. Once Mum said it was because I was a girl and was too short – I'm 130 cm! It's annoying and embarrassing.'

All young women need independence from their parents for their psychological and social development. One side-effect of today's tendency to bubble-wrap girls is that they can feel trapped and will escape in any way they can. And increasing numbers are making their escape via cyberspace, which is largely unsupervised: while they may be prohibited from walking to the local supermarket, thanks to the internet they can communicate with anyone and everyone in the 'safety' of their own home. A more rational approach seems to be in order here.

Regardless of the facts, many girls live highly orchestrated lives (they are driven to school, for example, instead of taking public transport) – the so-called 'bubble-wrap generation'.

Family changes

Nearly one in two marriages in Australia now ends in divorce. While the inevitable psychological dislocation is often handled constructively by both parties, many struggle. In addition, one in four Australian families are headed by a single parent, and while many of the affected offspring do very well, research does suggest that growing up in a single-parent household increases the risk of mental health problems in young people. We also have a rise in OINKs (One Income, No Kids) and DINKS (Dual Income, No Kids), a percentage of whom may have little or no involvement with young people and so indirectly contribute to the falling number of potential mentors for young people lacking access to adult guidance.

With at least half a million young people (or more) moving between two homes each week, the problem of fractured families is often further complicated by lashings of parental guilt. Some parents seek to 'make it up' to their children by creating a culture of indulgence – hesitant to use language that reflects their values or to set limits, which are basic tenets of good parenting. Adversarial parents may also become locked into a popularity contest, leaving their offspring with no moral compass – instead indulging in what I call 'Tamagotchi parenting', where all basic needs are met instantly but there is little love, guidance or wisdom provided (see chapter 4 for more about this).

To put it another way, as US satirist P.J. O'Rourke has done, many parents treat their daughters like dogs: 'Give a puppy her own set of house keys and put her in front of the TV instead of taking her for a walk. Let her eat anything that she wants and house-train herself. Send her to another master for visitation at the weekends and when she comes into heat, turn her loose in the pound.' As I've already said, many young people are making decisions today that their parents used to make for them; they are being left to their own devices by the adults in their lives long before they get an opportunity to rebel, as previous generations did. If you feel you might be straying down this path, take some parenting classes if you have to, and learn how to get involved.

'The reason I'm not too strict with my daughter is that I had a really strict upbringing myself and I hated my parents. I don't want my daughter to feel that way about me.'

I've heard this sort of thing from quite a few parents. But it's not a good idea to try to be a 'cool' mum or dad: it's your job to be a parent, not a friend. You may find it hard to believe, but your daughter is more likely to feel resentful towards you in the long term if you fail to set any limits at all and simply let her have her way on everything now.

Increased peer contact

This is the most tribal generation Australia has seen, in that they have unprecedented access to each other 24 hours a day via mobile phones, SMS and the internet. Previous generations had to limit their socialising to the (shared) family phone, or wait until they got to school or the weekend came around. Digital technology has also given today's adolescents much more privacy, as their communications take place out of earshot, and often out of sight, of their parents. Their peers thus become a 'second family' and often a young person's most precious resource, thus weakening traditional parent–child links.

The prevalence of recreational drugs

Binge-drinking and illicit drug use among young people is higher today than ever before. Many health professionals believe that girls who feel good about themselves are less likely to take drugs and, similarly, argue that the more miserable young people are the more likely they are to abuse drugs in some form of self-medication – in other words, to kill their psychological pain. Some experts suggest that the use of recreational drugs by young people with a genetic propensity to mental health problems is responsible not just for an increased prevalence of these disorders but also for the fact that they are occurring in much younger people. (For more suggestions about this knotty topic, see chapter 6.)

Under-fathering

Many girls today lack appropriate and constructive male role models in their daily lives. Fathers may be absent, present only irregularly, or simply unavailable emotionally, owing to family breakdown or because their lives are focused on their career and/or material ambitions. With a greater focus on individualism, more and more fathers lack Professor Parker's community 'mooring posts' and are retreating instead to the pub or club. In some cases, long work hours have supplanted many traditional social, family and leisure activities. In the safety of therapy, some men confess that the traditional family set-up in which they find themselves has become a barrier to achieving their hopes, dreams and aspirations, especially that of accumulating wealth.

Girls in a father-free situation may come to rely on alternative, often unbalanced, models of masculinity, which abound in the media and popular culture. Such models too often illustrate characteristics such as difficulty expressing feelings, concern with power and status, homophobia, anti-authoritarian bravado, and the reduction of sex to a 'sport'. Even where a male role model is available, he is often out of touch with the new social realities girls are faced with at school and beyond. In some families and communities (including schools), notions passed on to girls about appropriate masculinity are often still based on outdated, unequal power relationships between men and women. There is much that needs to be done about this, both at home and in schools.

That's all very nice, you may be thinking. But even if I can see that this is why things have changed, it doesn't necessarily help me know how to understand, let alone handle, my resident princess. Well, the following chapter has some suggestions to offer.

Chapter 3

Enter Princess Bitchface

Do you have a princess in the house?

The story of Nirvana on page 46 is an extreme example of the Princess Bitchface Syndrome, but from my experience it is clear that this sort of situation is not unique. At one end of the spectrum is the mild-mannered irritant who displays quite normal teenage behaviours. At its most extreme, the Princess Bitchface Syndrome is an acute disturbance of this natural phase of separation. But there are several techniques that are common to most adolescent girls.

Learnt helplessness

This involves acting helpless and dependent, so parents feel sympathetic and end up doing things for them – from homework assignments to chores around the house. Princess B effectively teaches her parents not to expect a whole lot from her, and may keep it up until she's had an apartment and car bought for her.

'My younger daughter Nirvana and I were always close, so much so that my friends used to joke that we were joined at the hip. Then when she got to secondary school everything seemed to change. She'd bring her school laptop home and would spend all her time in front of it talking to her friends. She wouldn't do anything around the house – even load the dishwasher or walk the dog – and would be rude whenever we asked. I tried to be strict with her (her father's a business executive and is hardly ever at home): I made a list of chores and put it on the fridge door, but I always ended up doing everything myself. Her father and I began to argue over how best to deal with the situation. I kept hoping it was hormonal, just a phase, but she became increasingly out of control. I'm just about at the end of my tether.'

However well-intentioned, Nirvana's parents are partially to blame for her behaviour. First up, her mother should stop doing the chores assigned to Nirvana. Both parents need to think about what it is that Nirvana values, and recognise that a (psychological) carrot is always going to be better than a stick. Smart parents take the things their children value and make these conditional upon things they don't value (like doing chores). In Nirvana's case it's internet chatting, so I'd suggest that the computer be made unavailable for a time. Nirvana has to learn that when she chooses bad behaviour, she also chooses the consequences.

The chore dodger

Princess Bitchface will avoid household jobs by telling her parents that she has too much homework, or an important test the next day. Alternatively, she will simply organise her life so that she is conveniently absent when she knows it is time to do things such as the dishes or cleaning up.

Keeping up with the Joneses

This tactic is designed to appeal to parents' competitive and social sensibilities by telling them that 'everybody else' has got a particular model of mobile phone or an iPod, and/or is allowed to go to the upcoming music festival. This is the time-honoured 'If you really loved me . . .' technique and seeks to induce parental guilt.

Divide and rule

A particular favourite of mine, this is where Princess Bitchface, having observed for a while the pattern of interparental dialogue, picks out which is the weaker parent and channels all requests through him/her. Once that parent is hooked this is used to induce cooperation from the other, who doesn't necessarily agree but does not want to be seen to spoil the party.

The ambit claim

This involves making an absolutely outrageous request, which when refused results in feigned disbelief at how unreasonable the parents are being. This exchange can last days, raising the emotional temperature in the family to boiling point; then at the last moment, in an apparent conciliatory gesture, she suggests a compromise (which was the real goal all the time). It usually appears in the form of 'Well, if I can't do that, can I at least do this?' Parents are often so battered by the debate they accede to this request.

The distractor

This technique involves choosing a moment when one or both parents are distracted or really busy, and then asking permission for something. Often the parents aren't even aware what they've given permission for, as they weren't really paying attention.

The debater

When confronted, or attempts are made to hold her accountable, she drags her parents into an endless debate by deftly mounting an argument that changes the focus from her behaviour to theirs. Typically she will point out how inconsistent, imperfect and hypocritical her parents are.

The terminator

This involves a pattern of issuing threats that she knows will push her parents' buttons: 'I'll run away from home', 'I'll kill myself',

'I'll ring the child protection service', and so on. Parents are so terrified that something dramatic will happen that they invariably give in.

So how and why does this more-or-less trying transformation come about? And, more importantly, what can you do when the tidal wave hits? Often, in working with parents, I give them this Parent–Daughter Power Quiz, asking them to tick either Yes or No for each of the following questions.

I can prevent my daughter from going out	Yes	No
I can choose my daughter's friends	Yes	No
I can make sure my daughter studies hard	Yes	No
I can prevent her from smoking and drinking	Yes	No
I can stop her listening to loud music	Yes	No
I can prevent her from using illicit drugs	Yes	No
I can prevent her from having sex	Yes	No
I can prevent her from getting pregnant	Yes	No
I can stop her from drink-driving	Yes	No
I can make sure she goes to university	Yes	No

If they (or you!) answer 'Yes' to any of the questions, I have to tell them they are living under an illusion. Parents have no genuine power over what their adolescent daughters like or feel, where they go, or what they do when out. This fact does not, however, stop parents from continuing to attempt to gain the ascendancy using an assortment of weapons including laying guilt trips, grounding, humiliation, shouting, threats, and character assassination. Yet the truth is that such techniques achieve nothing more than short-term, superficial and limited control, while at the same time running the risk of reaping aggression, insurgence and/or estrangement.

On the other hand, armed with a developmental perspective (see chapter 4) and with accurate, up-to-date and reliable information, you will feel – and be – much more in control.

The war of the worlds

Central to the successful navigation of adolescence is the extent to which each young person's developmental timetable matches up with the expectations and demands of others. Adolescence has long been a tale of the conflicting pressures of family, school, peer group and the evolving inner self. Today the battle-lines are drawn in much the same way, but things are more complicated. The letters I receive as an Agony Uncle for a girls' magazine tell of the angst of being still only on the cusp of maturity and yet being expected to act and dress like a sexy adult – largely because nowadays they're effectively discouraged in numerous ways from being children past the age of 10.

One of the main complicating factors is the fact that every day our daughters are exposed, pretty much as soon as they can read, to a million and one billboard, TV and magazine ads full of sassy-looking young things and the latest 'It's Hot!' stuff to buy. Music videos/DVDs and TV soapies have been found to be linked to unrealistic body images among adolescent girls (and, though to a lesser extent, boys). Add to this mix powerful electronic media such as the internet and mobile phones, and it's easier to understand how today's adolescents are being catapulted at warp speed into a culture of entitlement and consumerism. And the silver bellybutton hoops, low-slung jeans and tough-girl necklaces are by no means the preserve of teenagers – witness merchandising such as the Bratzpack, which is pitched at girls under 10.

So the colliding worlds of Princess Bitchface are further confused by other external pressures as well. But an understanding of the conflicting worlds she inhabits simultaneously is useful for an insight into the competing demands on her – and the confused and confusing behaviour that results from this.

Around 40 per cent of Australian children aged 8–17 use instant messaging (the figure is 56 per cent for 13-year-olds), and most use MSN. Adolescent girls on average spend two hours more than boys online per month, and their usage of instant messaging is higher too.

Her family world

In the quest for emotional and psychological independence from their parents, adolescent girls may vacillate between their yearning for the safe dependence of childhood and their need to be autonomous, but more often than not the latter will win out and they may appear hostile and uncooperative. So in each household evolves a creature of light or a creature of darkness, depending on the way in which the adolescent deals with this separation – which in turn depends on a variety of factors including personality, intelligence and temperament.

In trying to deal with their unacceptable feelings of love for and dependence on their parents, some adolescent girls become stuck in a groove of conflict with everything and everyone in their orbit. This can result in a three- to five-year period of psychological warfare that can be frightening in its intensity. In the most extreme cases the family finds itself living with a girl on the edge, whose rebellion, in overdrive, fuels a pattern of self-destructive behaviour – an emotionally starved young woman who knows only *that* she needs, without understanding *what* she needs. And the more Princess B feels she is losing control, the more aggressive her physical and verbal behaviour tends to become. At worst, she will keep up a snide commentary targeting her parents, and in the process she will sus out their most sensitive buttons and press them over and over again.

More often than not the clash is greatest between daughters and mothers. Chalk and cheese are the principal ingredients of this conflict – mother and daughter, once so emotionally intertwined, suddenly find themselves on different planets. One is trying desperately to get answers and information, while the other rejects and/or ignores such overtures as if they are intrusive telemarketing calls. Usually the only parent who may escape for a while is the father. This is because, while adolescent girls can have good relationships with their fathers, with few exceptions the attachment to their mother is far stronger and therefore they must be far more negative in order to deny the potency of that tie. So, teenage girls are generally able to maintain closer connections with their fathers (assuming that Dad hasn't, in the face of this familial warfare, beaten a retreat to work or the pub), who are accordingly often in a better position to negotiate a cease-fire, especially if they use youth-friendly communication.

If it seems at times that her friends are more important to her than you are, that she can talk more easily to her schoolmates than to you, it is because her friends give her a sense of identity and help her along the path to independence so that she will ultimately be able to function on her own. Thus friendships are pivotal in that the peer group can act as a psychological anchor while she is separating from the old ties.

'My daughter and I always seem to be fighting these days. She's sometimes so pigheaded and rude that I can't help getting angry and yelling. Nine times out of ten she loses it too and just yells back. It's like a vicious circle.'

It's not at all unusual for teenage girls to fight with their fathers. But to say that you can't help yourself isn't true: it's a matter of choice. You can choose to respond by yelling, in which case she will just do the same. If you really want to change the pattern that has developed, make a different choice – to walk away. Rather than responding in a negative way, simply say in a clear, non-aggressive voice, 'I don't want to argue right now. I'll come back when things have calmed down'. Try it!

There is some solace for parents trying to cope with this phase, in that all this adolescent insurgence is actually – as we have seen – a *normal developmental process*. Despite the 'disturbance in the force' that families characteristically live through, experience shows that most young people eventually adopt the values of their parents, and when they finally do so it is usually a more wholehearted acceptance than would have been the case if they had not challenged those views in the first place.

Her school world

At school, she also has challenges to face. It is about now that she must adjust to increased cognitive demands in the classroom. From the middle years the curriculum frequently includes more abstract, demanding material, and since not all adolescent girls develop formal thought processes at the same rate, this may be frustrating. In addition, she must expand her verbal skills to accommodate these more complex concepts and tasks, not only at school but also as she prepares for life as an adult. The limited language of childhood is no longer adequate. Some early adolescents may appear less competent than their peers because of their inability to express themselves meaningfully.

It is also at this stage that your daughter is expected to develop vocational goals. As part of the process of establishing her own identity, she is often asked to focus on the question 'What do you plan to be when you grow up?', to identify, at least at a preliminary level, what she wants to do and how she intends to achieve this. Given what we now know about brain development, this is both premature and unfair.

Problems can arise at school around this time when teachers and/or other staff forget that young women tend to develop sensitivity to control, and conflict is not uncommon.

On another level, for adolescent girls school is a social minefield – the daily setting for peer-group interaction. It's mostly about who has power and who doesn't, who's in and who's out, who's cool and who's not. Of course, schools vary and some cohorts within schools are amazingly civilised and develop an exceptionally positive ethos as the result of the particular mix of students in any one year.

'My daughter has just started Year 12. She's anxious already because she wants to work in the film industry and she knows it's an extremely hard field to get into. She has to do out-of-school classes as well as her normal school work, so she's spending much less time with her friends and says they are feeling hurt. What can we suggest to make her less stressed?'

The key to success in the final year of school is finding a balance between being focused, disciplined and working hard, and having time for a social life. If your daughter can establish a study routine, always studying at the same time and in the same place, her friends will come to know when she's available to socialise and when she's not. Letting them know that she is working to a timetable but has left times free to be with them is a vital step in allaying everybody's anxiety. If they are true friends they'll understand.

Often parents are unaware of how their daughters are treated at school or how they treat others, as some girls construct a social bubble around themselves as part of the emancipation process. As a result, parents may remain unaware of the nature and extent of their personal relationships until something untoward happens, such as them not sticking to a curfew, coming home drunk or stoned, or being assaulted.

Her peer world

Although peer interaction is not, of course, unique to adolescence, it seems to hit a peak of importance during the early and middle stages. The degree to which girls are able to develop stable and constructive friendships, and have an accepting peer group, is a major indicator of how well they will function and adjust in other social and psychological spheres.

The peer world of girls has been less of a mystery since Rosalind Wiseman's excellent book *Queen Bees & Wannabes* was published in 2002. Wiseman examined the factional groups that girls typically form, and the different, hierarchical roles within them. Such cliques can be found within every year level, within every school, to some degree. They function, according to Wiseman, like 'a platoon of soldiers who have banded together to navigate the perils and insecurities of adolescence'.

These cliques are where teenage girls learn about friendships and power. Depending on a girl's personality, temperament and emotionally maturity, this group can exert a major influence on who she does or does not talk to, which subjects she chooses, what after-school activities she engages in, her choice of boyfriend, how she wears her hair, and her values and beliefs – it can, in large part, determine her sense of self. For this reason, providing as it does a sort of second family, the clique can weaken the parent–daughter bond: it is likely to be the peer group, rather than parents, to whom girls turn when in trouble. Cliques also have a bearing on girls' relationships with boys. Having a boyfriend increases a girl's sense of self-worth and her status with her peers, although some girls will, in order to please a boy, sacrifice their friendships with their same-sex friends.

The relationships within the group are sophisticated and multilayered, and every member knows that her position is precarious and may change at any time. Ask the staff at any girls' school across Australia, and you'll discover that most year levels have one or two dominant alpha females who vie for power.

Wiseman's Queen Bee is most likely to be Princess Bitchface at home, as the techniques she uses to manipulate family members are the same ones she employs to control her friends. She invariably has good looks and charisma, loves being the centre of attention, can be extraordinarily assertive, and wields an almost hypnotic power over others in the clique. She seeks to weaken any potentially threatening alliances/friendships in order to strengthen her own power and influence. She will ignore and exclude anyone she does not deem worthy of being in her ingroup. She will often seek to destabilise peers by being nice to them one day and unpleasant the next, so that they never know where they stand. Another technique is to be particularly nice to one person as a means of snubbing another. Despite all these characteristics, she often slips under the adult radar and may be seen by adults as clever and charming.

The Queen Bee's position of power is maintained by a second-in-command described by Wiseman as the Sidekick, who dotes on and is ferociously loyal to her leader. The Sidekick tends to obtain her power and status directly from her association with the Queen Bee and generally adopts her 'look' and mannerisms. Together they intimidate and victimise other girls.

The next in line Wiseman calls the Banker. Smart, but usually quiet and apparently benign, she realises that information is the chief currency in Girl World and so makes sure she's always in the know. Her power resides in her ability to get others to confide in her. She is everyone's friend, while constantly 'banking' information that she can (and does) at some stage use to her own advantage. While she avoids overt conflict, if she plays her cards right she can become very powerful and a significant threat to the Queen Bee.

And so the hierarchy continues: there's the Messenger, the Floater, the Torn Bystander, the Pleaser/Wannabe and, of course, the Target – whose titles more or less speak for themselves.

A feature of interactions between adolescent girls is that any aggression is expressed covertly. While boys may act out hostile feelings and even come to blows, it is over quickly and usually

What to do if your daughter is in a clique?

The main thing to remember is that parents do matter. You might feel rejected at this time, but you are essential to your daughter if she is to navigate adolescence safely.

If you have a girl at the top of the heap, don't forget that those in a position of privilege don't like to be told they should change, nor do they believe there really is a problem. Affirm her, but hold her accountable: 'I love you, but I don't love your behaviour.'

Don't feel guilty. She's not necessarily a bad person and you're not a bad parent, but it is your job to point out what is going on and how it can impact on others. And be aware that being in the top clique can create a susceptibility to health-compromising behaviours such as early sexual activity and substance abuse. Bear in mind, too, that she no doubt knows this sort of life is a house of cards, which may cause anxiety. Remind her that popularity can come at a high price. There are advantages to being a Floater, for example, who is free to be genuine rather than living simply to please others.

that is the end of the matter. Girls are a different story – for them outright aggression is still considered unacceptable (the 'sugar 'n' spice' stereotype being alive and well, though physical abuse among adolescent girls is said to be on the increase), so she will rely more on psychological devastation: dirty looks, taunting notes and ostracism. The letters I receive at my magazine column suggest a consistent perception that expressing rage directly can result in the loss of relationships with others and that the prospect of isolation petrifies girls. There is an innate conflict between their feelings of anger towards their peers and their supposed social role as caretakers obliged to sacrifice their own needs for others. 'Cool' girls have lots of friends and typically don't involve themselves in direct conflict.

The fear of confrontation makes anger a circular issue that increases the scope of the conflict and causes girls to use relationships as weapons. Although the weak will more often be preyed upon, this sort of 'relational aggression' (the psychological term) is less about external characteristics and more to do with conflict that has not been addressed directly and openly. In other words, girls tend not to get closure on the conflict because they don't have the opportunity to express their anger in a healthy, fulfilling way. They must be 'friends', superficially at least, with everyone. As a result, resentments often linger, leading to grudges and, in some cases, future acts of vengeance. At home, the intensity of conflicts with parents can often be sourced to the pent-up frustration adolescent girls feel at school.

Her inner world

Now it's official: girls are more emotional, manipulative and moody than their male counterparts. Unfortunately for parents of more demanding daughters, female brains are predisposed to excel in language, auditory skills, fine motor skills, and attention to detail. Put simply, girl's brains are more decentralised, using a variety of parts or locations for a single task, whereas boys only use one side of their brain and process one thing at a time. Thus for adolescent girls the combination of biological changes, inbuilt brain programming, and external factors set the stage for a confused and at times tumultuous inner world.

After a year at high school Bec's new best friend was Kylie, who was more mature and sophisticated, and had become the single biggest influence in Bec's life. Kylie was the leader of the Cool Group, who were everything Bec wasn't but wanted to be. She soon dumped her primary-school friends, remade her look and began smoking cigarettes, going to elaborate lengths to hide this from her non-smoking parents. A clear picture of how this story could end is dramatically portrayed in the movie *Thirteen* – a must-see for any parent!

As we have seen, Princess B is in the process of establishing herself as an independent individual, while at the same time consolidating her own social relationships. In addition to a sudden spurt in physical growth, adolescent girls are able to think about their world about 18 months earlier than their male peers. Thinking about *more* things is a normal part of the maturing process, but a mature girl is also able to conceive of her social world with a new level of awareness.

On the one hand, she must develop a sense of her own identity. Up until now she has been chiefly an extension of her parents, but during adolescence she begins to recognise her uniqueness and, above all, her separateness from them. She must rethink the answer to the old questions, 'What does it mean to be me?' and 'Who am I?' This search for identity is one of the central tasks of adolescence. As the young woman matures, a new way of thinking about herself emerges. Identity involves developing a coherent sense of self that persists over time. According to the psychosocial theory of emotional development proposed last century by psychoanalyst Erik Erikson, and now widely accepted by many psychologists, identity must not only be perceived by the individual but also recognised and confirmed by others, especially peers. The less coherent this structure is, the more confused your daughter will be about her own uniqueness and the more she will need to rely on external sources to evaluate herself. Identity is dynamic, not static, and the formation of identity during adolescence sets the stage for continual changes through the adult years.

In addition, an adolescent girl must develop her own set of

values and morals. Ideally, during the early stages of moral development parents provide their offspring with a structured set of rules about what is right and wrong, what is acceptable and unacceptable – in essence, a moral compass. Then, inevitably, her parents' values will come into conflict with those of her peers and other segments of society. To reconcile such differences, she restructures her beliefs into a personal ideology. The pressure to rebel can sometimes be overwhelming, making this potentially a time of inner turmoil. It can be a total transformation.

The thought processes of Princess Bitchface

So the stage is set for an almighty confrontation between, on the one hand, a developing young female looking to test the limits and, on the other, well-intentioned but possibly under-informed and often inexperienced parents. What often ignites the pubertal powder keg is that familiar factor: brain-related complications.

All young people are prone at times to unhelpful, distorted thought processes, which often come to the fore when they are under extreme stress or if they are significantly depressed. It is as though adolescent girls carry an extra gene that promotes persistent negative thoughts, so that they often find themselves locked in a downward spiral that becomes more exaggerated as anxiety and/or stress increase. Encouraging young people to think about their thinking is very helpful. While adolescent girls are unlikely to discuss this with their parents, the website www.moodgym.anu.edu.au is an extremely useful tool.

'All or nothing' thinking

She thinks in absolutes – people, things or events are black or white, good or bad, with no middle ground. She tends to pronounce judgement using general labels: 'She's a slut', 'She's a loser ', 'He's a nerd'. She will condemn others on the basis of a single encounter or occasion.

Carmel's parents were keen to have her broaden her interest, so they took her to a local dance studio. She attended one class but then refused to return, saying that the school was 'gay' and she would never go back.

Catastrophising

She tends to magnify and exaggerate the importance of events, anticipating how awful or unpleasant they will be. She constantly predicts that negative things will happen, constantly overestimating the chances of a disaster. If she does suffer a setback, she will view it as part of a never-ending pattern of defeat.

Naomi is a Year 11 student who has a major test next week. Her parents know that she has studied hard for it, but Naomi is in a panic because she has convinced herself she will fail and that this will set the trend for this and her final year, and that she will probably die lonely and poor.

Negative focus

She focuses on the negative, ignoring or misinterpreting the positive aspects of a situation – or, indeed, the facts. She sees only the weaknesses of those around her, and forgets or ignores their strengths. If her parents do anything positive, she filters out and rejects this and focuses exclusively on the down side.

Charlotte has been trying to lose weight. She was 'good' all last week, but yesterday she blew it and had a piece of cake for dessert. She feels like such a loser! She's convinced she can't do anything right. She has spent the day mulling over the fact that she shouldn't have eaten that piece of cake. She's decided to go off her diet and eat the whole thing, then start the diet all over again tomorrow.

Jumping to conclusions

She interprets things negatively, even though there are no definite facts. She starts predicting the future and takes on the mantle of mindreader. She constantly predicts that bad things will happen.

Toni is giving a speech in front of her class. A girl towards the back of the classroom yawns, so Toni goes home convinced that it was a terrible speech and that the entire audience was bored.

Living by fixed rules

She tends to have fixed rules and unrealistic expectations, regularly using words like 'should', 'ought', 'must' and 'can't'. This leads her to be constantly disappointed and angry with those in her orbit.

Jane is kept waiting at school when her mother gets stuck in a traffic jam. Mum's mobile has died, so she can't call Jane to let her know she's running late. It starts to rain and with each passing second Jane becomes increasingly tense and angry. 'Why am I left standing here? Why didn't Mum ring? She's always late. She'd never do this to Priscilla (Jane's older sister) . . .'

Chapter 4

Some parenting principles

'The thing that impresses me most about America is the way parents obey their children.'

Edward, Duke of Windsor, *Look*, 5 March 1957

In some ways, it would seem from the Duke of Windsor's comment that things have not changed all that much. But in this scary, post-9/11, post-modern world, the challenges faced by young women and their parents are overwhelming and constant. The Princess Bitchface Syndrome could be seen as just one consequence of the fact that many young women are growing up lacking the firm discipline, support and nurturing they so badly need, especially at this time of their lives. While many parents have great intentions, it seems that an increasing number raise their teenage daughters via a curious mix of improvisation and hope.

Of course, all healthy teenage girls will test the boundaries once in a while – not least in order to ascertain where the boundaries are and to see if they are still being enforced. This is also an opportunity for parents to determine whether previously established boundaries might need to be adjusted.

But it seems that some otherwise-rational parents so indulge their daughters that they have lost sight of the demands being made on their time and energy, and of the challenging behaviours on display not just at home but also at school and in public places, from doctor's waiting-rooms to bus-stops and shopping malls. These parents seem to develop blinkers that can block out signs in their daughters of behaviour problems or even incipient mental-health disorders that can potentially exclude them from normal relationships with family and friends and at school.

When I misbehaved in my youth, my father just had to look at me in a stern way and I'd stop. Today's parents can look and look, because the average adolescent (male *or* female) will look straight back (and, as likely as not, roll their eyes). This, surely, is not the way things should be. We have arrived at a time and place where sometimes the fundamentals of parenting, in so far as I understand them – things like ensuring adequate sleep, good nutrition, exercise and fresh air – are no longer givens, because many parents hesitate to insist on them in case their offspring doesn't agree. Saying 'No' seems harsh or overly authoritarian. If we continue down such a path, we are failing in our responsibilities as parents to establish guidelines, to teach moral and ethical values. Worse, these girls will not learn problem-solving strategies, how to be responsible and to develop the internal resources to manage stress, loss, failure and disappointment (simple facts of life as we grow up), and so almost any bump in their road will knock them sideways.

What's your parenting style?

As I outlined in *Surviving Adolescents*, every adult has a parenting script they learnt when *they* were being brought up, which often governs how we parent our own offspring.

A parenting script has two main components: how *responsive* parents are, and how *demanding*. Being responsive means intentionally fostering a sense of individuality and self-regulation in your child; being attuned, supportive, and attentive to his or her special needs. The 'demanding' component (which is where many parents fall down) refers to the amount of control we exert over our children: it involves monitoring, providing adequate supervision, negotiating and consistently following through on a discipline system centred on the notion of accountability.

In some cases, unfortunately, the parenting scripts we follow or inherit are simply incompatible with the circumstances, like trying to use Windows 98 with XP. Social scientists have invented various names for the different parenting styles they have encountered, but they boil down to four characteristic approaches – indulgent, authoritarian, authoritative and uninvolved – each of which is the product not just of our own experience of being parented, but also of both parents' values and the practices and behaviours that flow from these. Here's my take on these styles:

- **Turtle** (indulgent) **parents** are more responsive than demanding. They are light-heartedly satirised in movies like the 2004 comedy *Mean Girls* (which was based on Wiseman's *Queen Bees & Wannabes*). These parents are easygoing, lenient, often unconventional, do not practise or expect mature behaviour, and allow considerable self-regulation. They avoid confrontation, and hide in their shell when conflict arises. Turtle parents can be conscientious, engaged and committed to their daughter, but their main aim is to be her best friend.

- **Rambo** (authoritarian) **parents** are commanding and controlling, providing a well-ordered and structured environment with clearly stated rules. They tend to be very decisive, but are not responsive – they seek acquiescence and immediate compliance, and expect their orders to be obeyed without explanation. They demand conformity, call for deference, and reward docility and dutifulness.

- **Watchdog** (authoritative) **parents** are both demanding and responsive. They impart and monitor clear standards for their children's conduct. They are firm, but not intrusive or restrictive: their disciplinary methods are supportive rather than punitive. They want their children to be assertive as well as socially responsible, and self-regulated as well as co-operative. They expect accountability and use consequential learning.

- **Tamagotchi** (uninvolved) **parents** are generally neither responsive nor demanding. They believe that once their daughter can fend for herself their job is to provide the necessities (food and shelter) but there is little or no emotional input.

One key difference between Rambo and Watchdog parenting is in the area of psychological control. Rambo parents expect their offspring to accept their judgements, values and goals without question. Watchdog parents, on the other hand, while expecting their children to behave appropriately and obey the rules, are more open to give-and-take and give calm explanations of the rationale behind the limits and boundaries.

A Watchdog parent:
- says 'No' when it's appropriate, even though saying yes would be much easier

- recognises that parents have rights
- is non-manipulative
- offers empathy rather than just sympathy
- encourages strength not weakness
- encourages free choice and the learning that comes from making mistakes
- uses consequential learning (which says, 'If you eat toast in bed, you must sleep with the crumbs')
- demands responsible behaviour

As you have probably gathered, I believe that Watchdog parenting is the most successful approach and results in happy young people. Even if you only start to practise it now (rather than in the early years, which is of course preferable), it may be more difficult but you will have a better chance of keeping your daughter safe (see chapter 6) and countering the development of the Princess Bitchface syndrome.

New times require new approaches

Most parents recognise that their style of discipline has to change when their offspring become teenagers. In childhood, children are free to love and depend on their parents and they are happy to let their mums and dads make all the decisions, but obviously the arrival of adolescence requires a different approach. It's much easier if you think of your role in terms of guiding them towards adult life and being clear about what the boundaries are, while not enforcing them in a dictatorial way. Giving a teenager an order or demanding that they comply is usually doomed to failure and can lead to battles that are best avoided.

The most successful parenting style is based on a 'developmental perspective'. This means thinking back to how you felt as a teenager and trying not to be too judgemental about your daughter's conduct, being tolerant about the mildly irritating behaviours that are common to young people.

Most adolescents will try out new ideas that may be unacceptable to their parents – this is part of the process of forming their own identity, rather than a deliberate attempt to annoy you. A warm relationship is ideal, but sometimes parents have to do things that their offspring won't like or understand. While some conflict and battles are inevitable, much of the low-level skirmishing represents a routine struggle for increased independence and autonomy. Your adolescent may, for instance, refuse to do something that seems to require very little effort: she drops her coat in the hallway instead of hanging it up; she won't write a thank-you note to a grandparent, however often you ask. Not only do simple things like this seem to her to demand too much exertion, but – much like a toddler – she has become very aware of her increased independence and widening range of choices. She says 'No' simply because she can.

It's a confidence trick

In a 2005 study undertaken by the Australian Childhood Foundation, 38 per cent of parents surveyed said parenting did not come naturally to them and 63 per cent were 'concerned about their level of confidence as parents'. Asked what strategies they used to teach children the difference between right and wrong, 98 per cent thought it was about making children feel loved, spending time with them, and setting a good example; 82 per cent favoured rewarding good behaviour; and 78 per cent said they reasoned with their children. All are admirable practices, but such an approach is unlikely to be effectual unless it is backed by firm discipline (which only half of the surveyed parents employed).

So why the decline in parental confidence? Why are so many parents afraid to set any kind of rules, limits or boundaries for their children? To me the answer lies in the permissive-parenting approach advocated by US paediatrician Dr Benjamin Spock in the 1950s and 1960s as a reaction against the authoritarian child-rearing practices of the past. The self-confessed insecurity of parents and their hunger for guidance indicate that these tactics simply have not worked. Many parents in the 21st century seem to be living in a vacuum of quiet desperation. The problems in schools as hapless teachers try to discipline kids whose parents can't (or won't) control them, and the pressure on doctors to pre-scribe drugs to regulate these children's objectionable behaviour, are symptoms of the problem.

Like British 'Supernanny' Jo Frost in her approach to younger children, I feel it's time to bring some old-fashioned commonsense back into the parenting of adolescents, to reintroduce notions such as 'unacceptable behaviour', 'right and wrong' and 'discipline'. Some childcare experts disapprove of the Supernanny's methods, but this is to some extent to be expected: after all, these experts could be said to have a vested interest, having largely replaced mothers, grandmothers and neighbours as dispensers of child-rearing advice. Yet the evidence suggests that their theories are the reason a generation of parents don't trust their own instincts.

Five key parenting principles

1   Parents have rights

Your daughter's transition from girlhood to adolescence can be a very trying time. The innocence of childhood gives way to opinions – a lot of opinions. As parents we are faced with obsolescence, in that *she* feels she is no longer in need of guidance, yet we still need to set limits and boundaries because her voice of reason is yet to develop. Put simply, parents have the right to point out that there are lines that aren't to be crossed and that if they are there will be consequences to be faced. All parents have the right (and obligation) to keep their daughters safe.

2   It's only a phase

It can be helpful to remember that we, too, struggled to find our footing gracefully. The passage from dependence to independence is awkward, to say the least, and rarely accomplished without some over-reaction by both parties. These feelings usually pass over time, but until they do you should avoid asking questions such as 'What is the matter with you?' and 'What's suddenly got into you?' Not only are these unanswerable, but they only aggravate the situation. Even if she does know what the problem is, she's hardly likely to say, 'Look, I am torn by conflicting emotions, affected by structural changes in my brain, engulfed by irrational urges and confused by raging hormones.' It's up to you to accept the behaviour as supportively but unobtrusively as possible, unless the manifestations continue over a prolonged period or seem severe.

The most important thing to keep in mind is (as illustrated by the mother's story at the beginning of this book) that this is just a stage, not unlike 'the terrible twos'. The reason the adolescent phase is harder to handle is the volatile mix of factors we looked at earlier (the mismatch of physical and mental development, parental guilt over being time-poor, peer pressure, media influences, the rise of the most tribal generation ever). The best way forward is for parents to learn to gradually relinquish control to its rightful owner, and for the young woman to learn to accept this responsibility without abusing it. However unlikely it may seem at times, the fact is that this emotional battle of wills will come to a natural, healthy end as your girl is replaced by the fine young woman she is destined to become.

3 Communication is the key

How you express yourself and what you say to your daughter, especially when you are angry, can inhibit your relationship with her. It's important, from the moment she is able to string two words together, to be able to talk to your daughter about every-day issues like school, sport, music and hobbies. If you don't talk to her about these things it will be harder for her to discuss the things that worry her later on.

And this is a two-way street: if while she is growing up she remembers you as always being prepared to listen (in a non-judgemental manner) without trivialising or over-reacting, there is a much greater chance of keeping the communication lines open. Try to lower your voice rather than raise it, and to maintain eye contact and, if possible, non-threatening physical contact. The only way your daughter will respect your views is if you value hers. By engaging in discussions about sex and drug issues at home, you will have more opportunities to offer guidance on the subject. (And to give good guidance on sensitive issues, try to be as informed as possible: see the Resources section at the end of the book.)

4 Disrespect is not proof of independence

Adolescents have not yet learnt the delicate balancing act of diplomacy – and be clear, it is a learnt art. If your daughter expresses her lust for independence by a lack of respect and consideration for others, inside or outside the family, this should not be ignored.

'My husband and I both have demanding jobs and we feel a bit guilty about often being home late and not having much "family life" with our 14-year-old daughter Mia. On the other hand, we figure she's doing better than a lot of other kids because she's pretty free to do what she likes, she gets plenty of pocket money and we often buy her a surprise to make up for not being around. But now a friend of mine says Mia's becoming spoilt.'

A lot of parents I see make this mistake – that is, they try to win or buy their daughter's affection and approval. This often seems to stem, at least in part, from a sense of guilt for not having enough time to spend with her. If you feel this might be happening in your household, redefine what taking care of your daughter means. Consider her emotional and spiritual needs: instead of using material goods to create a bond between you, make your-self emotionally available.

Disrespect is a sign not of independence but of immaturity (she is, after all, not yet mature). Accepting, let alone making excuses for, her bad behaviour will in no way help her find her psychological footing: you should respond in the same way you would to any adult who confronted you in an inappropriate manner. If she does not learn limits from her parents, she is sure to learn them much later, and much more harshly, from others in society.

5   Life is not a toothpaste commercial

Our primary job is to prepare our daughters for the real world. Not everyone has pearly white teeth, you don't always get what you want, and problems can't be solved by spending money. Your daughter does not have to love you every minute of every day – we all get over the disappointment of being told 'No'. But she won't find it so easy to get over the effects of being indulged: delayed gratification is part of adult life and she will be better equipped to deal with it later if she's been introduced to the notion while growing up.

Some years ago I read an article in the magazine *Nature* where scientists identified an epidemic of 'elephant breakdown', with large numbers of the majestic beasts suffering serious psychological collapse.

Poaching for ivory has slashed elephant numbers in Africa, and of those left a proportion are under five years of age, many of them orphans. In Pilansburg National Park in South Africa, young elephants began attacking rhinos. These juvenile delinquents had been raised by inexperienced teenage mothers left on their own to parent owing to a lack of older elephants. Gangs of hyperaggressive teenage elephants now roam the park: in one area 90 per cent of male elephant deaths are caused by other males – 15 times the normal figure.

Both elephants and humans can on occasions be intelligent, sociable and affectionate. There are other similarities, with elephants spending almost as much time as humans in childhood, living in tight matriarchal groups within which they form strong social bonds that last a lifetime. The young learn about the world from their elders, aunts and cousins. When they fail to bond or attach, the results are catastrophic. Perhaps we have much to learn from these creatures.

Chapter 5
Tried-and-true strategies

So, the secret is to give up trying to control your daughter. It's no longer desirable, let alone possible, to order her to do things – this will only bring about battles and even more resistance.

Hopefully, if you don't engage in conflict, she'll eventually realise that being cooperative isn't a threat to her independence. If, for example, she never tidies her room, there'll come a point where she feels so frustrated at not being able to find things (or simply needs some space to entertain her friends) that she'll have a massive clear-up. You need to accept that she has the right to deal with her own room in her own way. If you lead by example, keeping things elsewhere in the house well organised and tidy, the chances are that she will eventually do the same. (It also must be said that some adults have a double standard, accepting a level of chaos in their own domain but nagging their offspring to keep to an unrealistic level of tidiness.) You have to learn to let go, to allow your child privacy and space and the right to learn by her own mistakes. A sensible parent understands this, and avoids turning everything into a huge issue.

Living with Princess B

If you have got this far into the book, you will have realised that unlike my father's (and, indeed, my own) childhood – when parents generally told their offspring what to do and expected them to obey – in this changing world, young people (female and male alike) want to have a say in the decisions that affect them.

Being a parent today is difficult. On one hand we're responsible for our children, but at the same time letting them learn from their mistakes and experiences is an important part of helping them grow up. There are more than two and half million teenage girls in Australia today. While most don't share their parents' taste in music or hair-care products, or their belief in the need for common courtesy, the vast majority are reasonable and law-abiding citizens who treat their elders with at least a modicum of respect. There are some, however, who indulge in negative, attention-seeking behaviours that are challenging to say the least; and others (in the minority, happily) who exhibit consistent disrespect with a mixture of verbal and, occasionally, physical violence, especially when challenged. All parents are entitled to a decent quality of life and if your daughter's behaviour interferes with that, you have no choice but to act. This is not a licence to respond in a bullying manner, or to use sarcasm or put-downs – no matter how tempted you might be. All adolescents have an inbuilt sensitivity to being belittled and this will only escalate the emotional temperature.

Top 10 tips

Over many years of advising the frustrated parents of adolescent girls, the following seem to be my most consistent suggestions. In many cases, it must be said, the issue is as much about extinguishing certain parental behaviours rather than remoulding your daughter's!

1   Negotiate the rules

The best approach is for you and your daughter as early as possible to draw up *together* any rules that relate to her safety (relating to sex, alcohol, drugs, curfews, sleep and study). In this way she will feel she has some ownership of the arrangements and is more likely to adhere to them. State clearly what the boundaries are, but be prepared to negotiate and review them from time to time – the ideal is a gradual loosening of the reins, where you reward compliance with greater freedom. You might, for instance, insist that a 14-year-old be home by 10 p.m., but extend the curfew each year thereafter.

2   Use consequential learning

A consequential environment will teach your daughter self-control and self-discipline. Consequences should be agreed beforehand, and should be fair and reasonable, as too severe an outcome will invite her to rebel. (In other words, don't go overboard: if she breaks a curfew, for example, she might have to stay in the next night but not for the next month). The system should be used to change behaviour, not to make you feel better by getting revenge. And do make the consequences natural or logical whenever possible: with a prepaid mobile rather than an open-ended account, if she over- uses it and keeps running out of credit, she'll find she won't be able to text her friends; if she continually leaves her belongings all over the house, they may be picked up and placed in the freezer and/or a 'butler' charge may be deducted from her pocket money. (There is a special delight in seeing your daughter heading off to school in frozen shoes!) When the consequence fits the crime, she is much more likely to associate the two and remember them. Problems arise when we seek to protect our daughters from even the most benign consequences, or interfere with logical ones, so they don't learn the lesson of natural cause-and-effect but rather that we will rescue and take responsibility for what happens to them.

3 Don't be a doormat

Nowhere is it written that parents must provide their daughter with a mobile or an iPod, must spend money on her or give a reason for not doing so, must pick her up on demand, must drive her or her friends anywhere – in fact, spend time or effort on any-thing at all – let alone for someone who cannot be polite or who is outright abusive (even if you're told that 'everyone' uses that sort of language). In fact, to protect our own belongings, space, time, effort, money and dignity, we parents need to have a notion of ourselves as separate human beings and a sense of self-worth and self-respect. This is necessary not only for our own mental health but to model these qualities for our children.

4 Always say what you mean and mean what you say

If you say you will do something and you do it, or you say you won't do something and you don't do it, you will win your daugh-ter's trust. In the same way, if you say you will do something but you don't do it, or you say you won't do something and then you do it, she will learn you are not to be trusted – you will have no credibility and she will start to ignore everything you say. Follow-ing through is the means by which you delineate the limit beyond which you will not let your daughter go. Inconsistent parenting is a special kind of psychological death.

5 Use non-verbal management strategies (NVMS)

Most adolescent girls become immune to our verbalisations, so the best way round this is to do something rather than talk about it. Simply turning off a TV or disabling a computer is far more memorable than endless 'state of the nation' speeches that all blend into one. With NVMS she is likely to be caught off-guard and not be able to muster sufficient objections or negotiate her way out of the situation. Non-verbal parenting demonstrates that actions speak louder than words – and, better still, leaves you with more energy for more enjoyable pursuits.

6 Focus on the positives

Trying to eliminate undesirable behaviours – in other words, teaching her not to do things (for example, borrow things without asking) – not only opens up an infinite range of behaviours that you don't want her to engage in, but also involves endless monitoring for the undesirable behaviour just so you can draw attention to it. It is a basic rule of behaviour management that paying attention to a particular behaviour reinforces and is likely to increase it. Instead, decide what it is you want her to do and then state this in positive terms; tell her what you want, not what you don't want.

7   Use the 'Trudeau' approach

The late Canadian prime minister Pierre Trudeau invoked the War Measures Act in 1970 in response to terrorist activities by a breakaway group. This caused some consternation among journalists and civil libertarians, and one reporter asked him 'How far will you go?' Trudeau responded with 'Just watch me!' This needs to be your response when your daughter challenges you with 'You can't make me'. (Fortunately, like most parents, Trudeau was never tested to his limits.) Though we know deep down that we can't actually make anyone do anything, as parents we should never underestimate our own abilities – or, at least, our offspring's belief in our abilities. If she sees you as trustworthy and credible, she will believe that you are willing to follow through, even if she has never actually seen you do so. Aim to sound convincing, hold your head up high, make eye contact and don't 'blink' first.

The Godfather approach

This is nothing to do with concrete slippers or sleeping with the fishes. If you reach some impasse, why not make your daughter an offer she can't refuse, in that the alternative is so horrible that she will voluntarily choose the option you want her to. An adolescent girl would never choose 'awful' over 'pleasant', but she may well prefer 'awful' to 'even worse'. As an example: 'You have a choice – if you log out of the internet when I ask you to, you may be allowed to go back on next time you want to. If you don't, I will remove your laptop and it will remain off for a week.' In this situation it's most likely she will opt for the lesser of the two evils on offer.

8   Keep calm

When disagreements or out-and-out conflicts arise, don't respond in an irritated or angry way. Instead, remain calm and lower your voice rather than raising it – you don't have to yell to prove yourself. The more you shout, the more she will yell back. Adolescents generally, but girls especially, can't be controlled by authoritarian methods such as demands, orders and threats. A calm, consistent and united parental approach will usually reap the desired result. Having a 'robust discussion' out of the house is a great idea. And hard as it might be, try to remember that when she acts as if she hates you, it's more that she is upset and confused, or angry at your attempts to control her.

9   Make her accountable

As long as she is living under your roof, make it clear that she must be accountable for her actions, that you do have a right to monitor what she does and where she goes. However much you trust her, it's plain crazy to let her loose on the world all at once without any boundaries. At the same time, when negotiating what she's allowed to do and where she's allowed to go, you initially need to believe that she will behave in a judicious manner and to let her know that you trust her and expect her to respect this.

10 Act with conviction, confidence and dignity

Yes, this sounds like a tall order, but the last thing a girl needs is parents who are afraid of her or who act as unpaid servants. In these situations kids become intoxicated with the power this gives them, even though they may superficially appear to be working very hard to achieve it, because in fact they do not have the skills, knowledge or experience to handle it. When parents show that they don't know what to do, that they have no power, or that they are scared, her natural response is to become stressed and frightened herself. With many of the girls I see, this results in an escalation of their acting-out behaviours in order to force their parents to resume their parenting role.

Establishing the house rules

Many parents harbour real fears that their daughters will suffer some calamity if they are permitted to go out with friends, attend concerts, date boys and so on. In the old 'Children should be seen but not heard' days, it was the norm for parents to impose rules on their children. The conventional contemporary wisdom is that it is more effective for parents and adolescents to negotiate rules and sanctions *together*. To many parents this is an alien

---

Do your house rules need updating?

It's a good idea to reassess the house rules from time to time, to see if they're still useful and relevant. Here are some good questions to start with:

- Does our family have too many rules?
- Do we feel as if we're always telling our daughter she's done something wrong?
- Do we feel more like behaviour monitors than co-members of the same family?
- Do we find ourselves in power struggles with our teen?

If the answer to these questions is 'Yes', it might be that some of the rules need to go. In some families, as the girl gets older, new rules keep getting added but old ones don't get deleted. It makes for tired parents and frustrated young women.

concept – almost as if they're capitulating to their offspring. But, as noted earlier, the reality is that young people are more likely to stick to an agreement if they have been invited to participate in constructing it.

Rules are needed in every family so that everyone knows what is expected of them. This makes the world predictable, and therefore safer. Girls should know exactly what is expected of them, such as when homework should be done, when beds should be changed, what time they should be home, with whom they can share car rides, whether they should be earning their own spending money (and during what hours they can earn that money), and what contribution they should make to family life.

Base the rules on family values

Family values will inevitably influence the house rules. For instance, in some families it would be important for the whole family to attend religious services together; in others it might be optional. Some families might have more laid-back rules than others do about pocket money, parties or housework. It's important that we parents review our values to see if they really are values or just traditions. If they really are values, teenage girls will benefit from having rules that reflect them.

Involve your daughter in creating the rules

Although, as discussed earlier, adolescent girls still need a great deal of guidance, they are young adults and want to use the skills and the status they have attained. They want to have some influence over their lives. If your daughter is complaining about a rule, it might be worth your while inviting her to talk about how she would like to see that rule changed. It is crucial to put the onus on her to convince you: if she offers a thoughtful argument in favour of changing her curfew from 10 p.m. to midnight, say so and agree. If she fails to convince, you can tell her so but suggest that she feel free to come back later with another argument. At least she will feel listened to and less inclined to enter into the characteristic power struggle over this issue.

Make sure the rules are enforceable

There is no point having rules that you have no ability whatsoever to enforce, such as rules about who your daughter may associate with at school. Sometimes parents have so many rules that they couldn't possibly have time to monitor, let alone enforce, them, which almost always guarantees that she'll be able to circumvent them. It's better to have a few rules that are always enforced than many rules that are enforced haphazardly or not at all. The same goes for the sanctions when a rule is broken: grounding your daughter for a month, or banning the internet or TV for two weeks, might seem like a good idea but is virtually impossible to police. When sanctions are excessive, not only is she likely to forget what her crime was but she will focus her hatred on you. When sanctions are awkward to implement, you run the risk of not following through, following through intermittently or just throwing in the towel.

Spell out in advance the consequences of not following the rules

Consequences should always be known in advance. If they are not clearly articulated and anticipated they are seen as punishments, which doesn't teach your daughter anything except to avoid the punisher (and, no doubt, to develop revenge fantasies). If there are too many rules, it's hard to keep track of what the consequences should be, which is another argument against having too many rules. Rarely should a teen be 'grounded': if she comes home later than the agreed time, you can 'respect her decision' to stay home the next night. Having agreed consequences for infractions will help her to experience the positives of more freedom, more responsibility and less parental control.

Keep the rules relevant

It's also important to consider whether existing rules are really needed, or (as with family values) whether they are based on tradition-without-consideration. For instance, when your children were younger it may have been the rule that they cleaned their rooms every Saturday morning, because you were teaching them about organisation and hygiene. That system might need to be negotiated once your daughter (or son) reaches adolescence, as if they haven't learned hygiene by now they aren't going to learn it by entering into a power struggle about their room. Even if they have learned organisational skills, it might be more important that they use these on homework and time management than on keeping their room neat.

It will take time to relearn the parenting script you inherited and to confidently implement these new strategies. Many of them may appear obvious, but under stress good sense can be forgotten. Parents are allowed to make mistakes: the trick is to learn from them and not to make the same ones over and over again. Give yourself time, and do remember that most young people are very forgiving.

Chapter 6
Keeping her safe

Sometimes it seems as if it would be easier to keep our daughters safe at home until they turn into responsible adults. But if we did that, they'd never grow up – how could they, if they've never learned to cope with the world they have to live in? Yet, although it's impossible to keep an eye on teenagers all the time, it's important to always know where they are. It's also good to get to know your children's friends as well as their parents – and don't hesitate to check with other parents if you want to make sure your children are where they say they are.

Today there are all sorts of things that parents can become fearful about as far as their daughters are concerned, such as bullying at school and peer pressure at an ever-earlier age to undertake high-risk activities. In addition, as adolescence is a time of great physical and emotional change, increased stress and increased peer pressure, mental health problems can also occur. Let's look at some of these, and the best ways of handling them.

Bullying, girl-style

The chief form of bullying in Girl World is described by psychologists as 'relational aggression'. It is based firmly in cliques (see chapter 3) and simply means the ways in which girls manipulate the social scene to hurt selected peers. Spreading rumours, telling lies, revealing secrets and 'the silent treatment' are all forms of relational aggression. This sort of psychological cruelty has both short- and long-term consequences. So what can be done about it?

When talking to adolescent girls about their experience of intense bullying, I've often asked them what they wish their parents would do to make their life easier in such situations. Many feel their parents have not taken their concerns seriously, trivialising their pain with platitudes such as 'It's just a phase; it will pass' or 'She's just jealous'. These girls wanted someone to name the nature and extent of the loss, to honour their pain for what it was – disturbing, distressing and shattering. It's hard for parents to just listen and to hold their daughters, but that's exactly what these girls say they want. The trouble is that research suggests that up to 50 per cent of victims will tell no one.

Some dos and don'ts

- **Do** listen and feed back. Ask her about her relationships with other girls, then be quiet and pay attention. Reflect back to her what you hear, confirming it with statements such as 'Lisa's been your best friend for so long. That must have hurt.' Show your empathy by sharing your own stories and experiences. Do persist if she rejects your overtures, and don't take dismissals ('What would you know?' or 'I don't care anyway') at face value: she may simply be trying to dull the pain. Keep asking questions, and stay connected.

- **Do** help her to devise strategies. Often an understanding ear is all she needs from you, but do give help if she wants it. If, for example, she is being picked on as she walks home alone, suggest she walk home with friends. If she wants to confront her aggressor, discuss the best way to do it (pick a time when both girls are alone, not with friends) and role-play it a few times.

- **Do** teach her to be assertive. One of the best ways to stop gossip is to confront it early. Suggest that your daughter approach someone who's spreading gossip and say something like, 'I don't know if this is true, but I heard you said this about me, and I want it to stop.' Practise with her before she does so.

- **Do** encourage success. Girls who excel in some arena, whether it's sports, art, academic studies, music, drama or another field, are less susceptible to aggression than other girls. Self-esteem doesn't drop from the sky, they get it by being good at things.

- **Do** challenge her own attitudes. Acknowledge the pervasiveness of gossip – after all, it is a form of intimacy. How long can she go without gossiping? Could she and her friends journal their gossiping (who gossips the most?)? This is both tangible and eye-opening to adolescents. It is also a way of chronicling abuse.

- **Do** empower her. Remember that kids themselves are our most powerful weapons; teens listen to other teens. Encourage her to stand up for victims by not jumping on the bandwagon: she can help effect change by doing simple things like refusing to be an 'audience' for a bully, walking away, not gossiping or participating in on-line hostilities. Not going along with the abuse does not necessarily mean publicly standing up for the victim. A first step is to stand outside the tide of aggression, which may encourage others to do so too. Once people stop participating, the dynamics change – often the abuse just dies, or it can be publicly challenged.

- **Don't** trivialise her pain. Comments like 'It was probably just a joke' or 'She can't be a real friend if she behaves like that' all miss the point. They only prove to your child how out of touch you are.

- **Don't** intervene with the bully's parents unless it's absolutely necessary. This is sure to embarrass her and suggests you don't have confidence in her ability to handle things herself. If you must intervene, begin discreetly, with someone at her school who you're comfortable about approaching.

Approaching school when your daughter is being bullied

This is not easy, not least because describing events secondhand is difficult, particularly since most of these acts are subtle and indirect forms of aggression. In addition, many parents find it difficult to express their concerns and tend to be either very apologetic or too aggressive; they may also engage in character assassination of the girls in question, rather than focusing on their behaviour. It's all too easy in such situations to get labelled an 'hysterical parent' who is overreacting to her daughter's social shortcomings. A smarter approach is to document your concerns via an email to the teacher, copied to the year level co-ordinator and/or deputy principal, with a request to meet. At the meeting, calmly discuss with the teacher your concerns about what is happening, and ascertain whether he/she was aware of the interaction and the impact on the victim. If the situation continues after the meeting, seek a discussion with someone with more authority. Among other things, ask if your daughter can switch classes, because a great deal of social chemistry, particularly in school, forms along classroom lines.

Sex matters

If most episodes of *Desperate Housewives* leave you wanting to cover your daughter's eyes and ears, you aren't alone. Yet, research suggests that TV and other media are today a chief source of sex 'education' for children. And it seems that adolescents exposed to sexual material are more likely to become sexually active at a younger age. For example, Professor George Patton of Melbourne's Centre for Adolescent Health estimates that about one in five young people are having sex before they are 14. While a 2002 La Trobe University survey found that adolescent knowledge about sexuality and sexual health was generally good, it also revealed a worrying connection between alcohol and sex, with more than one in four sexually active Year 10 students (girls and boys) saying they were drunk or drug-affected the last time they had sex.

Here, as in most situations, communication is the key. Never miss an opportunity to talk with your daughter about sex. Remember, research also tells us that girls who feel they can talk about sex with their parents – because their parents speak openly and listen carefully to them – are less likely to engage in risky behaviours than are those who feel they can't discuss these things at home. An uncomfortable moment in a TV soapie could lead to a great discussion about puberty, peer pressure or even love; a news item might raise the topic of drug abuse.

Make sure you share your values about sex with your daughter. Many people feel very uncomfortable talking to their offspring about sexual matters, but the more you examine the subject the more confident you'll feel discussing it. Always try to answer any questions honestly and appropriately.

Many girls gradually become more self-conscious each year, so the earlier you do all this the better.

Dos and don'ts

- **Do** make sure you make a connection between sex and love, using everyday events in the family, such as a wedding or a birth, to discuss love and responsibility to others.
- **Do** respect your daughter's growing need for privacy – most become extremely embarrassed about nakedness (yours as well as their own).

- **Do** demonstrate that you trust your daughter to behave responsibly in sexual matters. This should act as an incentive for her to live up to your expectations. Constant prying or suspicion will have the opposite effect.

- **Do** give clear information about behaviour that's appropriate in any sexual situations – emphasising that her body is private and no one has the right to do anything she doesn't want or to make her feel uncomfortable. Giving your daughter this information early means that she'll be less vulnerable to abuse.

- **Don't** mock her 'crushes'.

Drugs

One of the great fears of any millennial parent is that their daughter will become involved in and/or dependent on drugs – licit or illicit. Studies show that in Australia around 25 per cent of 15-year-old girls smoke, and that more girls than boys smoke regularly. Alcohol seems to be the preferred drug, and National

Drug Research Institute figures in 2005 showed that two-thirds of adolescents aged 14–17 drink alcohol and more girls than boys drink to harmful levels. Cannabis use is also on the increase among adolescent girls, and national studies show that the average age when young people first try marijuana is 12.

As with sexual matters, use any opportunity you can to discuss drugs and drug use. Establish clear family rules about illegal drugs. Most importantly, explain to her what to do if someone offers drugs to her.

Many parents, not surprisingly, are frightened and confused about drugs. TV coverage of the issue has tended to exploit this fear, serving only to increase everyone's anxiety levels. Yet it is our role and responsibility to pass on accurate and up-to-date information about drugs to our children; engaging in endless emotional dogfights over the issue is unhelpful and potentially counterproductive. One way of passing on this information is to involve your daughter in an informal quiz (see page 133), perhaps even in the car while driving somewhere – or over dinner, which is an opportunity to involve the whole family. The idea is to find out how much you and your daughter really know about keeping safe and to impart some key messages in a youth-friendly manner.

Girl behaving badly

Isobel, who is 17 and lives with her parents, dropped out of school a year ago and is now doing a pre-apprenticeship in hairdressing. Every Friday she goes nightclubbing with friends; she usually doesn't get home till the early hours of the morning, by which time she's often drunk and drug-affected. She doesn't help at all around the house and has begun skipping classes at TAFE. On the few occasions her dad has tried to reason with her, she has withdrawn to her room or put on a 'floor show', becoming angry and abusive. Her personality seems to be changing and her mother, who hates conflict, implores her father not to confront her.

If Isobel continues to refuse to obey any of her parents' reasonable requests to share the household chores, come back at an agreed hour and to stop her illegal behaviours (under-age drinking, illegal drug use), despite warnings, then I believe it is perfectly acceptable for her parents to grab the reins. First, they should remove the privileges Isobel takes for granted (access to TV, internet and family car, and/or having her mobile bills paid), until she complies with her parents' requests. There is bound to be a war of attrition, especially if their parenting has been inconsistent in the past. If they do nothing, they are in effect supporting Isobel's lifestyle. On the other hand, intervening may help her get her life back on track.

Even if, as can happen in extreme cases, Isobel threatens violence or damages property as a response to the introduction of sanctions, her parents must not back down. My belief is that they should issue a warning that any violent behaviour will result in their calling the police – and, if the behaviour continues, follow through. While the police dislike responding to domestic violence calls, Isobel must learn that behaving in a socially unacceptable way has societal consequences.

Dos and don'ts

- **Do** arm yourself with reliable and up-to-date knowledge about drugs and drug use. Forewarned is forearmed.
- **Do** approach the topic rationally rather than emotionally. Harm minimisation is a more realistic approach than zero tolerance. As we have seen, at this stage of her life a blanket ban is unlikely to work.
- **Do** lead by example. Some 60 per cent of young people say their parents are the chief influence on whether they drink or not, and parents who drink are more likely to have children who take up the habit.
- **Do** help her to avoid people and places that may trigger drug use.
- **Don't** be moralistic. Preaching, like trying to control her, tends to inspire rebellion.
- **Don't** panic if she comes home drunk or drug-affected. Ensure her physical safety and help her recover.
- **Don't** condone regular drinking in the first three years of high school.
- **Don't** try to engage in conversation if your daughter is affected

by alcohol or drugs. Wait till she sobers up, and then get the facts.

- **Don't** hesitate to let her know you don't approve, and that if this becomes a regular pattern she needs to get professional help, starting with a visit to the GP.
- **Don't** smoke in front of your daughter.

Eating disorders and other psychological issues

The most crucial warning signs of mental distress or illness are social withdrawal, loss of interest in things that used to give one pleasure, trouble sleeping, decreased appetite or changes in energy levels. The altered behaviour is likely to be significant if it lasts for more than a couple of weeks – rather than being a temporary response to a minor setback such as a particularly bad week, a romantic breakup, failing to make the netball team, or not getting the mark she hoped for in an assignment – and is interfering with her ability to function.

Eating disorders

Anorexia nervosa affects 0.5–1 per cent of young women; bulimia, 1–5 per cent. There are several factors that affect eating behaviour during adolescence, including changing body shape and increased self-awareness, new sexual feelings, and risk-taking tendencies. In addition, of course, there is the ubiquitous media imagery that encourages unrealistic body images. Among adolescent girls in 'developed' countries, eating disorders are the third most common health problem behind obesity and asthma. While the proportion of the population that is overweight is increasing, young people are surrounded on all sides by images of 'ideal' but impossibly thin body shapes.

Eating disorders: some warning signs

- a marked increase or decrease in weight with no medical cause
- the rise of abnormal eating habits such as severe dieting or secretive bingeing
- an extreme preoccupation with weight and body image

- compulsive or excessive exercising
- self-induced vomiting, or excessive use of laxatives, diet pills or diuretics

Young people with an eating disorder are often 'in denial' and will most likely reject offers of help, preferring to isolate themselves. She may be on the constant lookout for opportunities to covertly exercise and to hide food rather than consume it – which can be infuriating.

Dos and don'ts

- **Do** remain composed and always talk calmly.
- **Do** seek professional help.
- **Don't** blame yourself or your parenting.
- **Don't** blame her for what is going on. And never give up on her, however difficult things get.
- **Don't** comment on her appearance. Whatever you say, it's likely to be misinterpreted.
- **Don't** try to force her to eat, or make mealtimes a major drama.

Depression

Research suggests that one in five young people suffer from emotional problems distressing enough to justify seeking professional help. The symptoms can range from relatively mild feelings of depression and anxiety to severe distress and dysfunction. Any such condition impacts on her ability to get through her day, and, worse still, can erode the foundation of relationships with family, friends and teachers. While clinical experience suggests that early diagnosis and prompt treatment are effective, many young people who experience a mental disorder never receive treatment for it. This is because many young people do not know where to go for help, and parents and teachers do not know what signs to look for.

Depression: some warning signs

- frequent, unexplained sadness or tearfulness
- persistent boredom and low energy
- a preoccupation with morbid or nihilistic themes
- lack of connection with friends and family

- extreme sensitivity to rejection or failure
- increased irritability, anger or hostility
- frequent complaints of physical illnesses, such as stomach-aches or menstrual problems
- a major change in eating and/or sleeping patterns
- self-destructive or self-harming behaviours

Dos and don'ts

- **Do** encourage regular exercise and sleep, and a healthy diet.
- **Do** seek help from a GP, and obtain a full physical examination with blood tests.
- **Do** try to engage your daughter in conversation, and listen carefully to what she says.
- **Do** encourage her to take part in activities that once gave her pleasure (walks, movies), and be gently insistent if your invitation is refused.
- **Don't** dismiss it as 'normal' adolescent mood swings.

- **Don't** disparage the feelings she expresses, but point out realities and offer hope.
- **Don't** accuse her of faking illness, or expect her to 'snap out of it'.
- **Don't** ignore any remarks about suicide: report them to her treating team (GP, psychologist).

TANDBERG

Conclusion: The fairytale ending

Adolescence is a confusing time of transition. No matter what kinds of pressures today's teenagers are under, the confused two-step of being yourself and fitting in wasn't invented yesterday, and it's not going to go away tomorrow.

The Princess Bitchface Syndrome is a serious social problem. This book is a call to arms, lest those problems worsen. Our teenagers are victims of the world around them: its materialism; its obsession with sex; its messed-up and ill-informed, though well intentioned, adults. The fact is that the chances of our daughters getting through it reasonably unscathed are slim if we don't pick up the reins and get involved.

Not many will argue that being a parent is one of the toughest jobs around. After all, there is no one way to raise a daughter who has become a tumble-dryer of physical and emotional turmoil while her designer clothes are being stretched every which way by rampant hormones egged on by the boy with tattoos and a troubled past. Each action, each word, each decision shapes a young mind. It's a lot of pressure and not even the experts get it right all the time.

The most common issues between parents and teens arise due to poor communication, power struggles and a lack of empathy. If you use the same parenting methods that you did when your daughter was a child, you won't get positive results. You'll just exhaust yourself.

So, give yourself a break. Family life has always been an ever-changing dance between children, parents, spouses, friends and the community at large. Embrace uncertainty, enjoy new dance steps and remember that each adolescent is an individual who has never done this before. Sometimes, things will be awkward. That's the human condition: it's normal and it's fine.

Alcohol and drugs:
how much do you know?

This section contains 10 brief scenarios, each intended to address popular misconceptions about drugs and alcohol. The idea is that you read out these scenarios to your daughter and her friends and see if they know the right answers. The most important part is to discuss the answers and consider key things you have learned.

The scenarios

Scenario 1

You've been at an 'after party' with your best friend, who earlier in the night had a fight with her boyfriend. She has been drinking all night and finally collapses. How would you know if she is just drunk or is suffering from serious alcohol poisoning?

Answer

If you pinch and/or shake her but can't rouse her, it is highly likely she is suffering from alcohol poisoning, so call 000.

Critical signs of alcohol poisoning:

- mental confusion, stupor, coma, or person cannot be roused
- no response to pinching the skin
- vomiting while sleeping
- seizures
- slow breathing (less than eight breaths per minute)
- irregular breathing (10 seconds or more between breaths)
- hypothermia (low body temperature), bluish skin colour, paleness.

Alcohol depresses the nerves that control involuntary actions such as breathing, the heartbeat and the gag reflex (which prevents choking). A fatal dose of alcohol will eventually stop these functions. After the victim stops drinking, the heart keeps beating and alcohol in the stomach continues to enter the bloodstream and circulate throughout the body. As a result, the following can happen:

- victim chokes on own vomit
- breathing slows, becomes irregular, stops
- heart beats irregularly or stops
- hypothermia (low body temperature) leads to cardiac arrest
- hypoglycaemia (low blood sugar) leads to seizures.

Even if the victim survives, an alcohol overdose can lead to irreversible brain damage. Binge-drinking (often the result of a bet or dare) is especially dangerous because the victim can ingest a fatal dose before becoming unconscious.

Scenario 2

You've been watching DVDs at your best friend's place. She's consumed far too much alcohol and is very drunk. Her parents are due home in two hours. Which of the following would be the most effective way to sober her up in time?

a) give her coffee
b) give her raw eggs

c) give her chilli peppers

d) give her a Berocca

e) put her in a cold shower

f) give her oysters

g) put her to bed and wake her up in 50 minutes

Answer

None of the above. Sobering up takes time. A little bit of the alcohol (about 10 per cent) leaves the body via breath, sweat and urine, but the liver is responsible for breaking down most of it and can only get rid of about one standard drink per hour. None of the above options can speed this up.

Scenario 3

A few years ago a man smoked 100 cones of marijuana in one day, approximately one every nine minutes. What do you think happened to him?

a) he went to sleep

b) he died

c) he became very paranoid, and beat people up

d) he threw up

e) he became very hungry and held up a fast-food outlet

Answer

(c) It was reported in the *Herald Sun* (14 February 2003) that a man was arrested after assaulting 12 people, including seven police officers, while suffering from drug-induced psychosis. It was estimated that he had consumed 14 grams of marijuana. Four canisters of capsicum spray and police batons failed to stop him. He was only finally subdued when he was given a general anaesthetic. It should be noted that this is a very extreme example and most people would not be able to smoke this much without passing out. This man had obviously smoked a great deal of marijuana and had developed a significant tolerance. The message is that marijuana is not a 'safe' or 'soft' drug.

Scenario 4

A guy goes to a party and is invited to play a drinking game where he has to drink a shot of vodka every minute for 100 minutes. He agrees to take part. Which of the following would be most likely to happen to him?

a) feels sick, goes home and throws up

b) feels sick, passes out and wakes up feeling awful

c) feels sick, passes out and goes into a coma for a week

d) feels sick, passes out and later dies

Answer

(d) It was reported in the *Age* newspaper on 23 February 1999 that a 19-year-old man died on his neighbour's lawn after drinking 88 nips and an entire bottle of vodka (four times the amount of alcohol required to cause alcohol poisoning). Your daughter needs to know that she can drink enough in one session to die.

Scenario 5

Your school has just decided to follow the lead of several private schools and subject all students to random drug tests. Your best friend is a marijuana smoker and wants to know how long traces of cannabis stay in her system?

a) 4 weeks

b) 6 weeks

c) 8 weeks

d) 10 weeks

e) 12 weeks

Answer

(e) Traces of cannabis and its active ingredient (THC or tetrahydrocannabinol) can be detected up to three to five days after one-off or occasional use. In a chronic user, however, THC can be detected up to 12 weeks after use (though the average is 25–27 days). Cannabis is highly detectable a long time after use because THC lingers in the fatty tissues of the body and leaks steadily into the blood and then the urine.

Scenario 6

A teacher at your school suspects that a student has brought some cannabis to school and goes to search her locker. Is the teacher breaking the law?

Answer

No. Desks and lockers are school property and can be searched without your consent. The only situation in which this does not apply is if you have paid a non-refundable fee for the use of your locker, in which case the school has no right to search it unless you have signed an agreement to that effect. If you have paid nothing, or a deposit that is refundable, the locker is school property and the school has the right to search it.

Scenario 7

If your boyfriend had a few drinks that took his blood alcohol level to .04, and he then smoked a joint and drove his car, his control of the car would be similar to someone with a blood alcohol concentration of:

a) .08

b) .09

c) .10

d) .14

Answer

(d) According to Dr Katherine Tzambazis of the Drugs & Driving Research Unit at Swinburne University's Centre for Neuropsychology, such an intake is equivalent to a .14 blood alcohol concentration. In such cases, reports show, your risk of having an accident is increased by 48. Watch what your driver is doing!

Scenario 8

You are at a party and a friend overdoses while using ecstasy. You go to call an ambulance, but another friend stops you – worried the ambulance officers will involve the police. Do ambulance officers call police in such situations?

Answer

No. Ambulance officers will not call the police unless there is a fatality.

Scenario 9

In young women, by how much does regular cannabis smoking increase the risk of being depressed and anxious?

a) three times
b) four times
c) five times
d) six times

Answer

(d) An Australian study found that frequent cannabis use in teenage girls predicts later depression and anxiety, with daily users carrying the highest risk.

Scenario 10

It's Friday night and you are at a club. Your friend, who does not drink much, seems completely off her head and you suspect her drink may have been spiked. What is the most commonly used drug in drink-spiking?

a) alcohol
b) rohypnol
c) valium
d) GBH

Answer

(a) Alcohol. A forensic study in the UK in 2002 following alleged sexual assaults found that around a third of the victims had consumed enough alcohol to make them pass out or suffer memory loss, and a further 24 per cent were drunk. Only 2 per cent of the samples taken contained sedatives.

Resources

I thoroughly recommend Rosalind Wiseman's book *Queen Bees & Wannabes: Helping Your Daughter Survive Cliques, Gossip, Boyfriends & Other Realities of Adolescence* (Judith Piatkus [Publishers] Ltd, 2002), which I draw on in Chapter 3.

The internet can be a curse or a blessing, depending on the reliability of the sites. You may find some of the following websites more than useful (all of them were active at the time of writing).

Bullying

www.bullyingnoway.com.au

This site provides a nationwide resource directed at minimising bullying, harassment and violence in schools. The project has been developed by education authorities as well as Catholic and independent school associations.

Drugs

www.druginfo.com.au

The DrugInfo Clearinghouse is a service provided by the Australian Drug Foundation. It offers free information, a specialist library, a telephone and email information service, and email-alerts.

General health

www.canteen.org.au

CanTeen is the national support organisation for young people (aged 12–24) living with cancer; including cancer patients, their brothers and sisters and young people with parents or primary carers with cancer. I must acknowledge an interest here, as I was involved in its foundation.

www.cyh.com/cyh/youth/how/how_index.stm

The South Australian Child Youth and Health site provides telephone numbers for the 24-hour, seven-day Youth Healthline Service for young people in South Australia. It also has links to parenting and child health information services.

www.rch.org.au/chips

Young people who develop a chronic illness during adolescence often have difficulty accepting their illness, and treating them can be quite a challenge for physicians. The Chronic Illness Peer Support (ChIPS) program provides valuable support for young people living with any type of chronic illness or medical condition.

Mainly for parents

www.familiesmatter.org.au

Families Matter has been developed as a necessary complement to MindMatters and seeks to engage parents, carers and families in the health and wellbeing of their young people.

www.fathersonline.org

The Fatherhood Foundation is a charitable, non-profit association that aims to inspire men to a greater level of excellence as fathers through encouragement and education.

www.parentlink.act.gov.au

An initiative of the ACT Department of Education, Youth & Family Services, which recognises and values the parenting role. Its confidential telephone information (02 6207 1039), advice, guidance and referral services are available to anyone who cares for children. The website has parenting tips and guides, information on community services and events, and some great links for parents.

www.parentline.com.au

Parentline (tel. 1300 30 1300) is a confidential counselling service aimed at providing professional support for parents and all who have the care of children. Available 8 a.m. to 10 p.m., seven days a week to parents in Queensland and the Northern Territory for the cost of a local call.

www.parentline.vic.gov.au

Parentline (tel. 13 2289) is a statewide telephone counselling, information and referral service for parents and carers with children from birth to 18 years. It is confidential and anonymous, and available for the cost of a local call throughout Victoria.

www.stepfamily.asn.au

This website aims to actively promote the positive aspects of step-family life, especially by providing appropriate information.

www.triplep.net

The Triple P – Positive Parenting Program is a parenting and family support service that aims to prevent severe behavioural, emotional and developmental problems in children by enhancing the knowledge, skills and confidence of parents.

www.parenting.sa.gov.au

Parenting resources and support aimed at helping parents in South Australia be their best. Site includes parent easy guides, state directory and discussion forum.

www.familycourt.gov.au

The Family Court of Australia website has great information including tips, forms and do-it-yourself kits.

www.justlook.org.au

Lifeline's national database of low- or no-cost health and community services offered throughout Australia. Note: it is not a counselling service.

www.i-dont.com.au

A service to assist people who are going through separation and divorce. The Relationship Separation and Divorce Directory lists organisations and others who can help.

www.lifeline.org.au

Lifeline Australia offers a 24-hour telephone counselling service for anyone, any time, and from anywhere in Australia. The helpline number is 13 11 14. From the website there's a link to MindMatters, which provides details of the centres interested in working with schools in their local areas.

Mental health

www.aacap.org/

The American Academy of Child and Adolescent Psychiatry site aims to assist parents and families to understand a wide range of developmental, behavioural, emotional and mental disorders affecting children and young people.

www.beyondblue.org.au/ybblue

Ybblue is a youth program of beyondblue, the national depression initiative in Australia. It is a very youth-friendly site bent on getting out the message that it's okay to talk about depression, and encouraging young people, their family and friends to get help when it's needed. The site includes interactive checklists, warning signs and symptoms, helpful contacts, treatment options, personal stories, e-cards and more.

www.blackdoginstitute.org.au

The Black Dog Institute (NSW) is the brainchild of the inspirational Professor Gordon Parker, who has put together a really informative website specialising in mood disorders. It has loads of expert advice on depression and bipolar disorder, along with advice on how to get help and stay well.

www.goodtherapy.com.au
This website outlines the various approaches in counselling and psychotherapy, and encourages visitors to explore what good therapy means to them personally. An advocate of making conscious, well-informed choices, the site has a directory of practitioners, public forum, articles and bookshop.

cms.curriculum.edu.au/mindmatters
The MindMatters program supports Australian secondary schools in promoting and protecting the mental health of members of school communities. Each state and territory has a dedicated web page.

www.headroom.net.au
Head Room – a cool-looking site dedicated to the positive mental health of children and adolescents and the adults in their life.

www.justask.org.au

Lifeline's Just Ask is a national mental health information and referral service specialising in self-help approaches to mental health. Visit the website or call 1300 13 1114.

www.livingworks.org.au

A suicide prevention scheme under the auspices of Lifeline Australia. Delivers programs that promote suicide awareness, increase practical skills in suicide first aid, and focus on follow-up help for people at risk.

www.kidsinmind.org.au

This website has been created by the Mater Child and Youth Mental Health Service (CYMHS), which helps about 1500 people every year. The site has dedicated information for children, adolescents and parents, providing a tool to exchange information and be informed about local, national and international issues in child and youth mental health.

www.eppic.org.au

The Early Psychosis Prevention and Intervention Centre (EPPIC) is a comprehensive service directed to young people aged 15–30 years who are experiencing, or who have experienced, their first episode of psychosis.

www.sane.org

SANE Australia is a national charity helping people affected by mental illness through campaigning, education and research.

www.friendsinfo.net/

The Friends website has information about the prevention and treatment of childhood anxiety.

www.miea.org.au

The Mental Illness Education Australia program aims to promote better understanding of mental health. Its services include presenters with personal experience of mental illness, who visit schools and community organisations.

www.index.agca.com.au

The MindMatters Plus Program Index provides summary details about a wide range of programs and resources that support students' wellbeing.

www.mcsp.org.au

Ministerial Council for Suicide Prevention based in WA. This site seeks to increase access to and availability of suicide prevention information for professionals, researchers and community members.

www.sfys.infoxchange.net.au

School Focused Youth Service is a federal government initiative designed to augment support provided to schools in response to the recommendations of the Suicide Prevention Taskforce.

Support for adolescents

www.cdc.gov/powerfulbones

A US site encouraging girls to take steps to improve skeletal health, especially by weight-bearing activity. It includes interactive activities and links to relevant websites.

www.4girls.gov

US site developed by the Office on Women's Health, providing reliable and current health information for girls aged 10–16.

www.dvirc.org.au/whenlove

A site for adolescents, with information and resources on relationships and self-esteem issues.

www.kidshelp.com.au

Kids Help Line is a free, confidential 24-hour telephone and online counselling service for young people aged between five and 18. There's a free quarterly newsletter.

www.lawstuff.org.au

This site provides a bunch of 'stuff' about legal rights for people under 18. It's sponsored by the National Children's and Youth Law Centre, an independent, non-profit organisation.

www.likeitis.org

This website gives young people access to information about all aspects of sex education and adolescent life, including contraception, 'lovebugs' (sexually transmitted infections), sex and sexuality, and peer pressure.

www.somazone.com.au

A program of the Australian Drug Foundation, this site was developed by young people for young people, with the aim of helping young people to address their physical, emotional and social health needs in a way that is relevant, non-judgemental and anonymous. It includes a question-and-answer service, publishes personal stories, and provides useful information on a range of youth services.

www.connectingkids.org.au

Connecting Kids Company is the trading name of the Peer Support Foundation, which was developed by health educator Elizabeth Campbell AM to provide a structured program for peer support in schools. The organisation offers a wide range of programs and resources, Australia-wide, and is based on the belief that young people can be empowered to help and support each other.

moodGYM.anu.edu.au

Designed especially for young people, this is an innovative, inter-active program aimed at preventing and decreasing depressive symptoms. MoodGYM, which teaches the principles of cognitive behaviour therapy, which has been found to be helpful for people with depression, offers services such as anxiety and depression assessments, relaxation techniques, and advice on dealing with stress and relationship breakups.

www.thesource.gov.au

This site has information on getting a job, career information, youth health issues and a Have Your Say section so the federal government can know what issues are important to kids.

www.reachout.com.au

A web-based program designed to inspire young people to help themselves through tough times. It provides support, information and referrals in an appealing format.

www.burstingthebubble.com

An adolescent-friendly site aimed at helping and supporting young people who have problems at home. It sends a very clear message that not everyone's family looks or acts like *The Brady Bunch*, or like the nice families on *Neighbours*, but that there are some things that should never change. It includes great quizzes to help young people understand what's normal stress and how to work things out.

www.makeanoise.ysp.org.au

This site is aimed at young people and contains information on a range of health-related matters including drugs, sexual health, mental health, school and money.

www.AngriesOut.com

This site was developed to give young people alternatives to conflict and violence when they are upset.

www.realitycheck.net.au

The aim of this site is to help young people make better choices about mental health. It provides information about where to find help in the ACT if you have mental health concerns.

Index